GRANDMA'S COOKING

GRANDMA'S COOKING

by
ALLAN KELLER

GRAMERCY PUBLISHING CO. • NEW YORK

Decorations by Rus Anderson

To
my mother, my aunt
and
my wife

Foreword

The recipes in this book, with a few exceptions, have been in my family for many, many years; most of them, in fact, for many generations. They were used originally in a day when care was important and haste was not. Since they were first copied down in Grandma's old, battered cookbook many changes have taken place in the kitchen. The wood stove is on the way out and the coal range not far behind it. Gas, electricity and even infra-red rays are now common fuel for the ovens of the mid-twentieth century.

One no longer tests the oven by thrusting the bared hand and forearm inside. Thermometers are accurate to a degree undreamed of by Grandma. Because of these changes the recipes have been modernized to be readily understood by today's generation of cooks. Yet not one basic recipe has been altered, so the resulting dishes will taste just as they did in the nineteenth century in the hills of eastern Connecticut.

These are not last minute recipes. Many of them demand considerable preparation and time, but the effort invested will be richly repaid in the entrancing appeal to the taste buds. Like any great masterpiece, a Yankee pudding, pie or roast is not dashed off in a trice. But when the lid is lifted and the aromas drift through the kitchen, it is like the spring that follows a hard, cold winter.

A.K.

Grateful acknowledgment is made to the New York
World-Telegram and Sun *for permission to use
certain material which originally appeared in
the columns of that newspaper.*

Table of Contents

PAGES FROM GRANDMA'S RECIPE BOOK

GRANDMA'S COOKING

Chapter 1

Grandma Cooked Like an Angel

MY grandmother was the best cook in the whole wide world.

There may be other ways of starting a story about Yankee cooking, but I think the truth is best. That is why I make a statement with which no one can quarrel.

People talk about Escoffier and all those fellows in tall white hats and with napkins knotted under their third or fourth chins but they weren't in the same league with Grandma. She took simple and inexpensive things and made them taste like ambrosia. Grandpa stayed in love with her until he was ninety-two, and that's proof enough. I don't mean he left her then. He just died.

When she put things like johnnycake and dried beef gravy, onion shortcake, Annadama bread, applesauce cake, baked cranberry beans, huckleberry slump or Old Connecticut peach pudding on the table, strong men wept—because they couldn't eat as much as they wanted.

On a hot day, when the men came in from harvesting, she'd have something like the huckleberry slump, with plain or whipped cream, for their dessert. In the winter, when the snow had drifted high along the sides of the house and barn up in Windham County, Connecticut, she would fix something like pork roast and onion shortcake.

She looked upon store bread as if it had been concocted by Beelzebub himself. Prepared puddings, cake mixes and other such aids for the city dweller and the woman who works had not appeared on the scene in Grandma's heyday.

Grandma lived at a time when ice came from an ice house. The pieces, cut from the fulling-mill pond the winter before, had been buried deep in sawdust in the double-walled, windowless ice house. There was no running water in the farmhouse, no electricity or gas or central heating, and what couldn't be canned in mason jars had to be kept, if perishable, in a cool root cellar or at the bottom of the well in a bucket, just above water level.

If the sweet old lady wanted apple butter she didn't buy it at the store. She made it the autumn before, peeling the fruit from morning until night of one day, and supervising its cooking in a great copper kettle over an open fire the next day. The cooking alone took from dawn until long after darkness had fallen, but hard work was something Grandma took for granted, like the killing frosts of November.

Parsnips had to be dug out of the ground from beneath the snow, and eggs were collected from nests in chicken houses that were so bitterly cold the combs and wattles on the Rhode Island Reds froze at night. It was Grandpa's job to lower the curtains in the coops when the sun went down, to keep out the icy winds; and he had to carry boiling water to fill the drinking dishes, or it would have frozen before the chickens could get enough to make eggs.

Every day, just before the shadows crept into the corners, Grandma cleaned and polished the glass chimneys of the kerosene lamps and lighted them one by one, putting them on the shelf behind the big stove, in the center of the table, and in the swing-away brackets on the walls.

Her kitchen was old, but clean as a whistle. The stove was rubbed and burnished with liquid that came in a bright yellow tin, and the random-width floor boards were as smooth as satin. There was a smell, compounded of burning birchwood, soup stock, home-ground coffee and spices, and coal oil that was as much a part of her kitchen as the old rocker, the range, the mantel clock and the Currier & Ives pictures on the walls.

Almost obscured by this smell was another, fainter, more feminine, that was born in Grandma's bedroom. It was there, with the help of heavy china pitcher, wash bowl, soap dish and hand-embroidered linen towels, that Grandma "freshened up" with water warmed on the kitchen stove and taken upstairs in a tea kettle, and a cake of transparent Pear's soap.

And it was there that the old lady kept her clothes and handkerchiefs stored away in bureau drawers and deep chests, in which packets of hand-picked and home-dried rose petals were added to perfume the garments. Sometimes Grandma took crab apples, stuck them with whole cloves, and hung them to dry behind the stove. When the last drop of moisture had gone from them forever, she laid them among the blankets, the aprons and the woolen scarves.

These scents—of Pear's soap, of rose petals and of spiced crab apple—fused into a perfume that clung to Grandma wherever she was, or whatever the season. Even the stout odors of the country kitchen couldn't drive it away or hide it.

Despite the handicaps, Grandma enjoyed life to the hilt and knew the pleasure of well-deserved leisure. She went to quilting parties and husking bees, played croquet so ardently that many a game was finished when it was so dark she had to tie bits of white cloth on the wickets to see where to aim, and she never said "no" to a picnic, or a strawberry supper or a stereopticon slide evening at the church.

In many a New England home there was a sampler, worked by young fingers, and then framed and put upon the wall. It read "God Bless Our Home." There wasn't one in the old house where Grandma and Grandpa lived. It would have been a little greedy. God had already blessed that home by putting Grandma in it.

When we were seated around the big table in the woodpanelled kitchen, tucking away food that would have excited kings and princes, I always wondered why men left the farm for the city.

I didn't myself—until Grandma went up to cook for the angels.

Chapter 2

The Man Who Brought the Mail

A LONG about the first week of December old Caleb Winchester, who delivered the mail at Grandma's, put his buggy into the carriage house and brought out his sleigh. Then we all knew that winter had come for good to Windham County.

Caleb's RFD route took him up Kick Hill past our place about noon, just when the children were floundering through the drifts on their way home from school for lunch. His two big chestnuts had to strain against their collars, and the breath came from their nostrils like puffs of fine smoke as they toiled up the steep grade.

There wasn't another vehicle like Caleb's in all of eastern Connecticut. It was a covered, box-like structure on sleds, with sliding doors on both sides so he could reach the mail boxes without dismounting, and a glass window in front. There was a small pot-bellied stove inside, behind the seat, and a little stovepipe that stuck up through the roof like a periscope.

Traffic was no problem in those days, so Caleb had no window in the back of the sleigh or a rear-view mirror. This made it perfect for us kids. We got so that we could appear as innocent as angels when Caleb drove by, sometimes even managing to look as if we were actually going in the opposite direction.

But the minute the mailman had gone past far enough to be unable to see what was going on behind him we'd rush and hitch our sleds to the rear of his sleigh and ride uphill in state.

If those big Morgans died prematurely of weakened hearts, I'm afraid every boy and girl in town must have shared the blame.

The inside of Caleb's mail sled was really something. He had pasted pictures from calendars, magazines and the Sunday papers over every square inch of the interior. Most of them were copies of Currier & Ives prints, dog heads from hunting magazine covers, and such like.

If Caleb were alive we'd let it rest there, but a lot of snow has fallen and melted since he made his last delivery so it won't hurt any to reveal that some of the pictures were downright racy.

There were brightly colored, life-like reproductions of sultry beauties from Cuban cigar boxes and a collection of well-padded females from Billy Watson's Beef Trust.

All of these latter pictures were on a part of the wall that was obscured when the door slid back. Even if a nosy woman wanted to look around inside to see if her mail-order corset or the package from the Boston Store was hiding under the first-class mail she would never be able to spy out Caleb's secret sin.

The rural mail carrier used to doze between farmhouses, and it was this habit that gave our town some of its more exciting moments of rustic history. Sometimes, while snoozing, Caleb would inadvertently let the reins go limp, and one of the horses would get a line caught under his tail. No horse can stand this, even one as docile and well trained as the mailman's. So when this happened, Caleb's nag would rear up, paw the air and take off, frightening the other horse into the same mad flight.

Usually the old codger would restore order before too much damage had been done, but often the coffee pot would spill from the contrivance that was supposed to hold it on the stove, over ruts and thank-you-ma'ams and through the drifts. Many a legal notice and store bill, even love letters, reached their owners dyed a rich, coffee brown.

The town selectmen made an earnest attempt to keep the roads clear, but it was before the day of modern machinery, and they didn't succeed all the time. After a heavy snowfall several farmers who owned oxen hitched their yokes to home-made plows, fashioned out of stone-boats with V-shaped flanges on the forward end. Several rocks were placed in the plow to keep it from riding up on top of the drifts and then the oxen were driven up and down the roads until most of the snow was piled along the fences, out of the way.

Oxen were better at this task than horses. They could pull harder and work longer, but better still, they didn't get skittish when floundering in deep drifts as the horses did.

If the roads hadn't been plowed out, the mailman had a

tough time getting through on his rounds. I recall one day after the snow had been dusting down heavily for many hours, Caleb reached Grandma's place with a badly winded, spent team. Grandpa insisted that the mail carrier stay overnight, wait for the storm to blow itself out, and go on the next day after the roads had been cleared.

Caleb hadn't been delivering mail all those years without knowing of Grandma's prowess with the bowl and spoon so he allowed himself to be persuaded. He drove the big Morgans into the barn, rubbed them down carefully, fed them, and blanketed them so they could cool off without being chilled. Then he stomped into the kitchen, his eyes aglow with anticipation and the crow's-feet around his mouth wrinkled up into a smile. He was lucky, sure enough, for that night we had Shipwreck, Apple Snow, and strong black tea.

Grandma made Shipwreck by slicing an onion into a large buttered baking dish, then covering it with a layer of raw potatoes, sliced paper thin. Next came a layer of chopped top round beef, a layer of uncooked rice, and another of chopped celery. Sometimes she added a layer of cooked red kidney beans. On top of that went three cups of cooked tomatoes which had been rubbed through a fine colander and blended with an equal amount of water.

She salted it and sprinkled a little freshly ground black pepper over it, put on the cover and popped it into the big oven. For two hours it cooked at a moderate heat. If it seemed to be getting dry, Grandma added a little water, but not enough to make it too moist.

Shipwreck was served from the dish in which it was baked and usually there was a side dish of Grandma's mustard pickles to lend an added zest. I used to wonder where this delectable concoction got its romantic name of Shipwreck, but the story behind it must have been lost years before the old lady made it a favorite repeater on our menus.

I can still remember Grandma making Apple Snow. She pared a large, tart apple and then grated it before adding three-fourths of a cup of powdered sugar. Using a very large bowl, she then put in the whites of two fresh eggs.

She used to sit in the armless rocker by the window that faced the road, the bowl in her lap, stirring the mixture tirelessly. Grandpa said you had to give this pudding Hail Columbia or it wasn't worth the bother, and Grandma surely did.

When it was light and quite stiff she served it in good-sized dessert dishes, piling it up in the center and pouring a soft boiled custard all around it.

There was cake to go with it, sometimes coconut layer and sometimes mocha, but always a cup of rich tea from Brownell & Field's spice and tea warehouse.

Old Caleb Winchester counted that blizzard as one of the luckiest events in his life and used to tease his wife about Grandma's cooking. At the time I didn't think anything of it, because every meal she put on the table was a sort of homespun masterpiece. I realize what a fool I was, now that Grandma is dead these many years.

Chapter 3

Holypokes and Quahog Chowder

ONE winter day there was a great bustling and scurrying at Grandma's, with the old lady putting on her bonnet, heavy coat and woolen shawl, and Grandpa hitching the bay mare to the Portland cutter.

A big soapstone was taken from the oven, wrapped in an old piece of carpet, and laid on the floor of the sleigh. Blankets enough for a regiment were piled in next; and the old couple climbed in, leaving just enough room, it seemed, for a boy barely into his teens.

So we drove down to the Central Vermont Station to pick

up Aunt Patience and her adopted daughter, Abigail, who were coming up from Mystic for a week's visit in the hills. This was before the automobile made visiting back and forth by relatives the common, uneventful thing it is today. In those days, a cousin's arrival from fifty miles away was more exciting than a visit today from a relative flying in from Singapore.

Grandpa kept the mare going at a brisk pace, and we slid easily along the road between high drifts that had piled up against the stone walls and the fence rows. The harness bells jingled, the mare's breath came out in white plumes, and the frosty air set the webs to forming in our nostrils.

The old man tooled the shiny, curve-dashed cutter to a slithering stop when we reached the station, both the mare and the sleigh-runners kicking up a powder of dry snow. It was at least twenty minutes before train time, but in the country no one shaved corners too thin at times like this. Better a whole hour early than a few minutes late, with some poor frightened female left to stand alone on an empty platform. It was warm under the blankets, with the soapstone sending up a kind warmth that reached clear to our waists.

Suddenly there was the deep-throated whistle at the crossing south of town, and then the train came huffing in to a stop, brake shoes grinding in a pinwheel of sparks and the engine spitting out steam and cinders.

First off the train was a mail sack, shapeless and limp. Next came Aunt Patience, as stiff and erect as the mail bag was not, and behind her, in a bright red coat, high buttoned shoes, fur-trimmed hat and muff, came Abigail, a vision of breathless beauty.

Somehow the three grownups squeezed into the cutter's single seat. Then Abigail and I jammed ourselves in among the blankets at their feet. I never figured out whether it was because the girl was so pink and pretty and eye-filling or whether it was because I was sitting on the soapstone but I was on fire from copper-toed shoes to woolen cap.

That afternoon Abigail and I went fishing for pickerel. We both put on skates when we reached the fulling-mill pond, and I chopped holes in the ice with a handaxe, rigged up lines and fastened them to tip-ups. Each device had a small piece of red flannel tacked to it so that when a pickerel hooked himself the tip-up would wig-wag madly to catch the attention of the fisherman.

The wind blew down off Wannagunssett Mountain and whipped across the ice as if each gust were edged with pinking shears. Abigail said she was afraid her face would freeze and that she had read Eskimos rubbed their skin with snow to prevent frostbite. That was all I needed. I'm afraid, looking back at it now, that I almost rubbed Abigail's cheeks raw, but she didn't seem to mind in the least.

We built a bonfire on a point of land that jutted out into the pond, feeding it with dead branches from the woods that stretched clear back into Pigeon Swamp. Every once in a while Abigail would squeal with glee when one of the red tip-ups showed we had a pickerel hooked, but she wouldn't touch the fish. By sunset we had a baker's dozen, frozen as hard and stiff as cordwood.

It grows dark early in Windham County in January, and before we knew it the blaze from the fire was the only light we had as we gathered in the tip-ups. It was so cold that before the last one was picked up, the first few holes had frozen over.

We put the fish and our skates into a burlap sack and sat huddled up close to the roaring fire. Anyone who saw us, although no one did, would have sworn we were sitting tight together just for warmth. Funny thing, though, neither one of us was the least bit chilly.

After a while we pushed the embers out onto the ice where they sizzled and went out. I lighted the coal-oil lantern, shouldered the sack and we walked home to Grandma's through Jabez Stetson's pasture.

Grandma had guessed when we'd return, right to the minute, and had a batch of molasses taffy all ready for pulling.

In a saucepan she had cooked a cup of white sugar and three-fourths of a cup of brown sugar, two cups of light brown molasses and a cup of water together, stirring it constantly over a slow fire, until the mixture started getting a little brittle. Then she had taken it off the stove, added a fourth of a cup of butter, an eighth of a teaspoon of baking soda and a fourth of a teaspoon of salt, stirred it again, and poured it into a buttered tin to cool just enough to handle.

Abigail and I washed our hands, smeared them well with fresh creamery butter, and started pulling the taffy, keeping at it until the mixture was a light, tawny yellow, and fairly firm. It was all Abigail could do to keep from being pulled across the kitchen and she giggled every time we doubled the rope and started tugging again. Finally we stretched it into a thin column, twisted it, and cut it into inch lengths.

Grandma knew that even kids having a hilarious time couldn't make a meal on taffy alone, so she had made a dish of what she called "cherry bread." She had filled a deep stoneware pudding dish with alternate layers of buttered bread and sour cherries, stoned, and stewed in sugar. She sat the dish out in the snow by the side door and the mixture half froze into a thick sort of jelly.

We ate it with a warm custard sauce, and both Abigail and

I went back for seconds. Then the cat jumped up into Grandpa's lap and both went to sleep. Grandma and Aunt Patience put their heads together over a bit of choice gossip and there was nothing for the two of us to do but go into the sitting room and—look at the family picture album.

Chapter 4

Everyone Wanted Peach Pudding

G RANDMA'S kitchen was a wondrous place. The big wood range kept it warm and cozy even when the trees were snapping with frost back in the woodlot. The old mantel clock measured time in easy, patient swings of the pendulum, apparently giving the old lady plenty of opportunity to prepare and serve the best food this side of Paradise. At least she never seemed to be in a hurry over cooking.

Next to the kitchen was the buttery, which city slickers call the pantry, and it, too, was a place of marvelous odors, bewitching sights and tangible evidences of the good life.

I can remember certain aspects of this chamber of gustatory delight as though I were looking at a photograph. On the left side of the buttery was the spice cabinet, a masterpiece of the carpenter's art. Behind the glass door were forty-nine bottles, well corked, holding whole cloves, anise, bay leaves, peppercorns, sweet marjoram, garlic salt, cinnamon sticks and all the other spices from far lands that went to change roasts and puddings from ordinary fare to items acclaimed by anyone who had the good fortune to eat them.

A lot of folks in Windham County took care never to miss such an opportunity. During the summer the Congregational Church had many covered-dish suppers on the lawn and when the church asked Grandma to contribute something everyone in town knew it would be one of her Old Connecticut peach puddings.

She lived not too far from the church so that the puddings were still warm when the parishioners tore into them. If Grandma had ever crossed up the committee and sent something else I think there would have been shooting in the streets of the village.

(The ingredients are listed on page 199.)

Grandma blended the sugar, egg yolks and shortening together with a few fast stirrings. Then she added the dry ingredients and lemon rind alternately with the milk. If you are perturbed by the double sugar entries in the post positions above, don't be. Grandma was a good cook and she could sense that the ingredients ahead of the peaches were going to be used at a different time than those after the fruit.

She'd rub the sides and bottom of a shallow baking dish with shortening, fill the bottom with peeled and quartered peaches, sprinkling them with two-thirds of a cup of sugar and lemon juice, then pour the batter over the fruit and bake it in a moderately hot oven for half an hour.

She made a meringue by beating the egg whites stiffly and patiently adding the powdered sugar. Back into the oven went pudding and meringue to stay for about fifteen minutes, just to brown the fluff on top.

This pudding was invariably served warm, either by itself or with cream. Quite often one peach stone would be left in while the pudding was cooking, but this was downright risky. While it certainly added a decided tang to the taste, there was always the great danger that it would be forgotten and do serious damage to Grandpa's store teeth.

Grandpa was right fond of soft molasses drop cakes which could be dunked in cambric tea at the end of the meal. Grandma kept them in good supply in an earthenware crock on the bottom shelf next to the gingersnaps and the sugar cookies.

To make them she creamed five tablespoons of shortening with a spoon until it was light and fluffy. Then she added a half cup of brown sugar firmly packed, creaming it in thoroughly. Next came a cup of blackstrap molasses or sorghum, stirred in well. She sifted a tablespoon of soda, a quarter of a teaspoon of salt and three and a half cups of flour together, and added this mixture alternately with a half cup of sour milk, stirring all the time.

I can still see Grandma dropping the batter by the tablespoonful on a greased cooky sheet and sliding the tins into a moderately hot oven, where it took only eight or ten minutes to turn the batter into slightly mounded, soft cookies with a surface that looked as if it had been stained with dark oak varnish.

When the kids came in from playing, the drop cakes appeared by magic, along with glasses of milk from the cellar or the well, where it had been cooling in the bucket. With a platter full of these drop cakes in front of you, and the stove, radiating warmth and comfort behind, life was a wonderful thing.

The automobile raised the deuce with good cooking. It made it too easy to go to the store, and good as the stuff may seem, what one buys in a store is never in the same league as the stuff someone like Grandma makes. But although Grandpa was one of the first in the county to buy a car (a two-seater Stanley Steamer), Grandma remained true to her heritage.

She refused to have any truck with store bread. This meant she had to bake her own, and being a woman of considerable imagination, she varied the recipes so that she made plain white one day, rye the next time she baked, and at other times graham, raisin and cinnamon bread. One of her favorites was called Amadama bread in our family.

The recipe can be found in old cookbooks in New England and sometimes it is called Annadama bread in those collections. According to the legend, a State-of-Maine farmer complained because his wife served him this special bread to the exclusion of all other types.

"Anna, damn her, won't make any kind of bread but this yere stuff," he said, angrily. From this remark came the local name for this loaf, and in time it was corrupted from "Anna, damn her" to "Annadama."

Grandma didn't care about the origin of the name. She took the recipe at face value and made the bread, altering the quantities a little to suit her own taste and finally wrote it out in her dog-eared, battered old cookbook.

(Her recipe is shown on page 153.)

The dear old lady added the corn meal slowly to the boiling water, stirring constantly. Then she added the shortening, molasses and salt, and after that, allowed the mixture to cool to lukewarm. She crumbled the yeast cakes in the lukewarm water and stirred that into the corn meal batter.

I can still see her adding flour slowly until she had a stiff dough, kneading it well on a floured wooden board. It was plumped into a greased bowl, covered with a clean towel, and left on the warming shelf of the stove to rise. When it had doubled its original bulk, Grandma took a sharp knife and cut through the dough several times, letting some of the pent-up gas out. Without moving it she let it rise again for forty-five minutes, then took it out and kneaded it well on the lightly floured board.

Grandma shaped it into two large, or three medium-sized, loaves, stuffed them into greased bread tins and put them back to rise, covered with the same towel. After they'd risen until they humped up an inch or so above the lip of the tins, she put them into a hot oven for ten minutes, then reduced the heat and finished the baking which took a full hour in all.

It's an easy thing today to twist an indicator on a gas or electric stove to reduce the heat, but Grandma had to monkey with the old wood stove to achieve the same ends. She'd leave the oven door slightly ajar for a few minutes or set the stove lids off center to cut down the draft, and she knew how to set the dampers to cut the fresh air down or step it up better than most engineers could handle a boiler room.

When the loaves were tipped out on a rack and the crust brushed with butter to keep it from being too hard, an aroma drifted through the kitchen that has no equal in today's cookery. If I had broken no windows playing baseball, or had a better than average report card, Grandma cut off a couple of hot slices, plastered them with butter and beach plum jam. I ate them unaware of my good fortune. The memory alone can start my salivary glands to overflowing.

Memory can play strange tricks, they say, but when it comes to remembering about Grandma and her surroundings, it is as if each item were etched on steel.

She moved about the house with cheerful decision, doing the things that had to be done without complaint, but finding time to do many other things just because they gave her pleasure, or made life more comfortable for others.

Each spring she hung a handful of twisted strings in the lilac bush beside the side door, so the birds would have something to build nests with. She always cut the pieces short so her little friends wouldn't hang themselves while weaving them in and out among the twigs.

When a new baby arrived it received a hand-crocheted afghan in soft wool, or a crib quilt, hand sewn during the minutes between popping things in and out of the oven or at the end of the day when the sun went down behind Obwebetuck Mountain almost before one realized it was mid-afternoon.

Grandma, like most country women, was closely concerned with the weather. She read the forecasts but didn't always agree with them.

"Frost comes six weeks after you hear the first katydid," she'd say. Or perhaps it would be, "The bluejays are hollering; we'll have snow by nightfall."

Behind the stove hung the current copy of the *Old Farmer's Almanac,* well thumbed by both the old lady and her husband. She followed the long-range predictions but only to see if they agreed with her own theories which were based upon the thickness of the caterpillars' coats, the moss on the north side of trees, and the date when the purple martins flocked together for their trip south.

Next to the almanac hung the turkey wing duster—a device for moving dust from one spot to another, not for getting rid of it. Grandma never used it, yet she wouldn't throw it out because her mother had used one and her grandmother had used one before that. She used a damp cloth and except when Grandpa was threshing, you couldn't find a speck of dust in the whole house. Then, with the whole air full of chaff, even the old lady couldn't keep up with the dust.

For a woman in her middle seventies, Grandma could certainly move around under a full head of steam. It's true that for long trips Grandpa could get the Stanley Steamer ready in a half hour or so, but for everyday affairs the old lady relied strictly on shanks' mare.

She thought nothing of traipsing "cross-lots," down Kick Hill Road, through the Wilson's lower meadow and across the spillway from the fulling-mill pond on a small foot-bridge. Then she climbed through the edge of Sheldon's woods and down on the far side to the grammar school yard and so to the other side of town. Had she gone by way of the crossroads at the store it would have been a little more level but much longer. And she was eternally in a hurry.

"Pshaw," she said one day when a much younger woman expressed dismay at her activity. "When I was in pigtails I played hare-and-hounds over these very same hills, dropping torn bits of paper to make a trail for the pack. It was very seldom anyone caught up with me. And in the winter I played fox-and-geese in the snow. Just because I've added a few years there's no cause for me to shrink away like a dry violet in the sun."

That was before the day of psychoanalysis and self-examination.

Grandma never had time for those things, and that's why she stayed hale and hearty, and as chipper as a school girl.

Chapter 5

A Kiss on the Covered Bridge

FROM the top of Kick Hill to the far side of the Shetucket River was four miles—all down grade—and with a good man at the ropes and ten or a dozen boys and girls to give it weight, a double-ripper sled could do it in what seemed like five or six minutes.

Windham County double-rippers were homemade devices. They consisted of stout boards suspended on two small sleds, one up front and one in the rear. By sitting well bunched together a dozen kids could sit on the sled with ease. If it was cold, everyone sat tightly packed for added warmth. If it wasn't so cold, you did it anyway because it was cozier that way. The girls just couldn't get away from you.

Most of the coasting was done in the evening, and if the moon wasn't out the only light was that shed by a small carbon lamp fastened on the front of the double-ripper. This fact, coupled with the bundling, made it easy to steal a kiss or two on the way downhill past the Kick Hill schoolhouse, Grandma's house and the depot.

If the girl was extra shy, and there were a few who were, you could wait until you reached the covered bridge over the Shetucket. In that long, black cavern the boy who couldn't wrestle a girl into one good, long buss didn't deserve to eat a big bowl of quahog chowder or salsify soup and a plate of holypokes at Grandma's anyway.

We used to "eat around" on coasting nights. We'd start with cider and doughnuts at one place and move on later to another. But invariably we wound up at Grandma's for soup and holypokes. She never minded the snow melting into watery pools on the kitchen floor, and she had a way of looking past girls and boys who were standing pretty close together in confused wonderment that never embarrassed them. Old as she was, she could remember perfectly the joy of making love while rushing down a snowy road at breakneck speed.

Grandma's quahog chowder had these ingredients: a small piece of salt pork (about ¼ pound) cut into bits; two sliced onions; three or four potatoes, according to size; a quart of boiling water; a pint of the hard quahog clams, put through a food chopper; the liquor saved from the clams; and freshly ground black pepper.

She tried out the pork until it was crisp around the edges, browned and tender, and then browned the onion in the same skillet. While this went on, the potatoes were diced.

Then these were put in the boiling water and cooked until the potatoes were tender. In went the quahogs and as much of the liquor as was needed to give the chowder the right taste. This was where care had to be taken. Grandma didn't want the chowder to be too salty. Pepper was sprinkled on, and the soup cooked until the clams were tender and soft.

In our house no one would have dreamed of eating quahog chowder the first day. It was put away in mason jars and allowed to season overnight. The next day it was reheated and milk and butter added while it was warming up.

The old lady always served holypokes with her chowder when the kids came in from sliding downhill. These she made out of once-risen bread dough by shaping the dough into balls the size of hazelnuts. After they'd risen again until about twice that original size she plopped them into her iron kettle of hot fat and cooked them until lightly brown. After they were drained on clean paper she served them with maple syrup on a hot plate alongside the chowder. Some used to pass up the syrup and dunk the holypokes in the chowder.

Grandma's soups were famous all over Windham County. One of her favorites came originally from my Aunt Freelove, who lived in Hop River, not far from Nathan Hale's birthplace. She called it the Hale Place Soup. It required a cup of dried split peas or an equal amount of cranberry beans; eight cups of boiling water; enough stewing lamb, cut in chunks, to cover a bread and butter plate; a tablespoon of rice; a carrot and two onions cut into cubes; a tablespoon of dried parsley and a big pinch of salt.

The old lady picked over the peas carefully, peering through her steel-rimmed spectacles to make sure no pebble got by to bother Grandpa's store teeth, and soaked them overnight. In the morning she drained them, added the other ingredients, and put them all in a covered bean pot. For five hours the soup baked in the oven of the big wood range, which was kept as low as possible.

Grandma served soup often during the week, but it never tasted as good as when the night's sliding was over and everyone wanted to get warm before the long walk home. After a couple of big bowls, a plate of holypokes and maple syrup or perhaps a few chunks of sage cheese and piping hot cocoa, zero weather had no terrors for a Yankee boy.

If he could hold his girl's hand tightly in his, inside the pocket of his Mackinaw jacket, and steal a kiss once or twice while squiring her home, who cared if the snow crackled crisply underfoot and the trees cast ghostly shadows in the moonlight?

Chapter 6

In the Parlor, in the Gloaming

THE door to Grandma's parlor was kept shut most of the time. There were too many things in it that small boys could break—things that seemed priceless and wonderful in an earlier, simpler world.

There was the stuffed horned toad from Mexico, resting on a slab of bark; a stiletto handed down, generation by generation, from the ancestor who saved his life by wresting it from a Spanish freebooter; and a photo album that played a little tune from Haydn as the leaves were turned. Then, too, there was the little bottle filled with water from the River Jordan— Grandma said; and best of all, the stereoscope.

In one corner of the room was a birch-wood cabinet filled with the thick-curved, double-view cards that were inserted in the wire guides of the 'scope. The viewer, with its glass lenses and the soft green velvet eye pieces, rested on the mantel shelf unless Grandma herself was there to see that it was handled carefully by small hands.

I can still remember looking at the Houses of Parliament in Ottawa, the towering crags of the Canadian Rockies, scenes from the Holy Land, blossom-encrusted views of Charleston's gardens, and the grave of Bobby Burns.

Talk all you will of Hopalong Cassidy or the Space Cadets, there will never be a thrill like watching Blondin tip-toe across Niagara Falls on a tight rope through the stereoscope that gave pictures a life-like third dimension. And when the tigress from the Cincinnati Zoo was only four inches away from your nose, the skin on your back fairly crawled with fear.

Older folks seemed to prefer views of Westminster Abbey and St. Paul's Cathedral, the cottage of Shakespeare's sweetheart in Shottery or the home of Walter Scott. We younger fry knew where the more exciting cards were filed. There was the cog railway up Mount Washington with the lady on the front seat patently dying of terror, and the Broadway horsecar that seemed almost to move.

After we'd looked at those, there was nothing to do but gaze upon Nelson's tomb, Washington's grave at Mount Vernon or Edward the Confessor's final resting place. Years later I read Oliver Wendell Holmes' comment that to an American it must seem as if all England is one vast burying ground. He must have been looking through a stereoscope when he arrived at that conclusion.

When a young man came calling on his lady friend in Grandma's time it didn't matter what pictures they looked at.

The stereoscope was a dandy device for huddling together on the horsehair sofa or the love seat. It was immaterial whether Robert E. Lee on Traveler was right-side-up or upside-down if the circumference of the girl's waist was just equal to the length of the boy's arm.

Grandma was an understanding soul. Sometimes she would come into the parlor at a time like that, coughing as if she had galloping consumption, or humming her favorite hymn, "Lead, Kindly Light," which gave the young sweethearts time to quit what they were doing and pick up the viewer. Then she'd turn down the wick in the big parlor lamp, the one with great red roses on the base and shade, mumble something about saving on coal oil, and disappear toward the kitchen to fix up a snack. That left the parlor in a dim, half-twilight where every shadow was love's ally.

After a bit the sweet old lady would return, banging doors, "scatting" at the cat—anything to make a racket—and bearing in her hands a tray on which all sorts of delicacies were mounded up like a great pyramid covered with a linen tray cloth.

Among the favorites were Sand Tarts. Grandma loved them and so did the children. To make them she let a half cup of shortening stand in a mixing bowl near the stove until it was soft. Then she added three-fourths of a cup of sugar, one egg, one tablespoon of milk and one teaspoon of vanilla. These she mixed thoroughly.

Next she sifted together one teaspoon of baking powder and one cup of flour and added it to the other mixture. Then she stirred in two additional cups of flour until the dough was stiff enough to roll. She rolled it out very thin, cut it into rounds with a cookie cutter, and placed the cookies on a well-greased baking sheet.

Just before putting them in a hot oven Grandma sprinkled them with a mixture of sugar and cinnamon, and cooked them about five minutes, or until they were a delicate brown. It was the brown appearance of the sugar and spice that gave the cookies their name.

Often there would be Lemon Honey Cookies on the tray. These would have made a Dresden china doll's mouth water.

For these she creamed together a half cup of shortening, a cup of sugar, one teaspoon of vanilla flavoring and a half-teaspoon of grated lemon peel. She added a well-beaten egg and two tablespoons of milk, and sifted together two and a half cups of flour and two teaspoons of baking powder, adding the latter to the other mixture.

This she made into a dough, rolled thin, and cut into rounds which were baked ten or twelve minutes in a moderate oven until lightly brown.

For the filling she blended carefully one tablespoon of corn starch and one-fourth of a cup of cold water, and cooked it until clear, stirring constantly. Next were added two table-spoons of butter, a cup of sugar and the juice of half a lemon. This was cooked until well thickened. A well-beaten egg was folded in and the mixture allowed to simmer for three minutes.

Grandma chilled the filling and then put the cookies to-gether, two by two, with the lemon filling forming sandwiches.

Sometimes there would be little Banbury Tarts on the tray, and at other times finger doughnuts, with a filling of wild foxgrape jelly, or little fried apple pies no bigger than a Cape of Good Hope stamp.

The old lady served hot cocoa or postum or cambric tea with the cookies, and I wonder if half the guests knew how lucky they were.

Chapter 7

Grandma Hisses the Villain

WHEN the dishes were washed and put away and the kitchen tidied up, Grandma loved to hitch her old Boston rocker over by the stove and read for an hour or so—if the mending was all caught up.

It was a time to which she looked forward all through the day—a reward for the arduous labors of a farm wife—when she could read of some Handsome Harry's downfall at the hands of the honest country boy who saved his sweetheart's honor from blemish.

When the villain was hissing his evil importunings into

the tiny shell-like ear of Marie, the upstairs maid, Grandma's chair behaved like the walking-beam on a sidewheeler steamer. It rocked forward and back under the old lady's impetuous urging but it also crept sideways, always in one direction, so that every now and again Grandma had to hitch the rocker back to the stove, where the process started all over again.

If things were really precarious for the always pretty and always innocent heroine, Grandma would get so excited the chair would wind up against the far wall of the kitchen where it would chafe against the baseboard until the annoyance broke through the old lady's composure.

Ordinarily she was calm and sweet-tempered. No one had ever heard her say a mean thing about anyone, or known her to be visibly upset by the small things that annoy most persons. But at such a time she'd come as close to exploding as she ever did.

"Land's sake," she'd cry in exasperation, "why in creation did we ever get rid of that platform rocker? It stayed put, more than you can say about this hobby horse."

A few minutes later she'd be deep in the romance again and the chair would be creeping inexorably toward the far wall.

Grandma laughed and cried over *To Have and to Hold* and *The Blue Flower*. She followed *Beverly of Graustark* from one mad adventure to another, and she shivered over *The Hound of the Baskervilles*.

One time Aunt Patience came for a long stay and brought several books with her from a store in New London. The two sisters could hardly wait to get things in order in the evening so they could pick up the novels again. Even a small boy could sense there was something unusual in their excitement. Ferreting it out was something else again. Grandma had left the other books around on the table or shelf, but two of those Aunt Patience brought were almost never out of their hands, or hidden somewhere for safekeeping.

Such whispering you never heard before. The books were passed back and forth so that the more exciting passages could be shared for extra enjoyment. Aunt Patience forgot all about her chronic indigestion, munching on nut-filled cookies, great wedges of pie and the like, late into the evening, with never a complaint. Grandma was so swept away with emotional exhilaration that one night she forgot to put the cat out and Grandpa had to get up to do it when the old pet protested by jumping on the bed and clawing at the quilt.

I wondered what strange sort of literary fare the two old ladies were indulging in, but I didn't get a chance to break through their guard until the afternoon Aunt Patience was preparing to take the Central Vermont train home. I got a quick glimpse at the titles as she was kissing Grandma goodbye. One was *The Garden of Allah,* and the other *St. Elmo.* Compared to today's lively novels, they appear rather diluted, watered-down items of escape, but that was another, gentler, era.

Grandpa had too little leisure for anything more than the weekly paper, the *New England Almanac* and the *Country Gentleman.* Grandma's personal tastes were considerably broader, but when it came to reading matter for a boy there was a definite rigidity of outlook. A good report card, or perfect attendance at Sunday school over a period of months, usually meant that Grandma bought another Horatio Alger or another G. A. Henty.

The old lady was mighty handy with needle and thread and used to make the sewing machine hum furiously, pumping on the foot treadle as if her life depended on it. She turned out most of the everyday clothes herself, but like most of her

Yankee neighbors, she relied on a dressmaker to make her go-to-meeting dresses, the draperies and curtains and finer things for the house.

The dressmaker was Miss Amanda Sweet, a prim, white-haired, straight-backed fence rail of a woman who spent the bulk of her days living and working in other people's homes. Automobiles were still rare and train service between country towns was notoriously bad, so Miss 'Mandy was picked up at one place, when her tasks there were done, and taken on to the next house or village.

I was at least eight years old before I learned that she wasn't one of the many old-maid relatives that always exist in a large family. She slept in the same spare bedroom used by our true aunts, ate whatever we ate at the same table, and took an intimate, animated part in the family conversations. Usually she stayed four days. Sometimes, if there was a graduation or a wedding imminent, she stayed five or six.

She wasn't penniless, but just as obviously she was a long way from well-to-do. Yet she always brought little gifts for the children of the households she visited. They were home-made, usually; things like doll dresses for the girls and gim-cracks for the boys. Once she made a football out of an old pair of corduroy knickers and stuffed it with rags. It was a dud so far as kicking went, but a broken field runner (aged seven or eight) could tuck it under his arm and never fear about its bouncing out if he were tackled.

Miss 'Mandy knew everything about nearly everyone in Windham County because of her peripatetic life, yet she never gossiped in an unseemly way, or said an unkind thing about one family to another.

"Miss 'Mandy is a perfect lady," Grandma said one day just

after the dressmaker had gone on to her next appointment. "I always say 'A dog that brings a bone will carry a bone,' and Miss 'Mandy brings nary a bone."

The seamstress rose at cock-crow, ate breakfast with Grandma and Grandpa (it was Grandpa's second snack), and then went briskly to work at the cutting table or sewing machine. She never soldiered on the job, and she stopped only for meals or a mid-afternoon cup of tea. In the evening, when she was free to do nothing, she nonetheless never sat idly by. Her gnarled fingers moved incessantly, and although she talked and joked and entered into the family fun, seams had a way of being sewn, tucks were put in and buttonholes were bound.

One time when she was visiting—we never thought of it in any other way—she made pillow covers for the pillows on the old horsehair sofa. I remember it distinctly because my part in the enterprise was such a large and important one.

For months I had been collecting and "swapping" with other youngsters to build up my collection of silk and velvet flags that came in the boxes with Helmar, Hassan and Turkish Delight cigarettes. It had been a tough struggle, in view of the fact that ten- and eleven-year-old boys didn't smoke, but constant watchfulness and polite attention to older relatives and friends who did smoke helped to build up the trophies.

There were flags of all nations, college shields, heads of Indian chiefs, and soldiers in gaudy dress uniforms. They were hoarded like hundred-dollar bills in a tin box that had once held Jamaica ginger candy.

Grandma thought the little bits of silk and velvet would look very handsome, pieced together with fancy stitching and made into pillow covers. There was an argument about it but Grandma, seeing how highly treasured the mementoes were, solved the problem with the wisdom of Solomon. She asked me to give up only the duplicates—the ones with which future trades might be effected.

This wasn't too bad except that at the very end of her work Miss 'Mandy found she needed one more piece of silk. It was like cutting off my right arm, but after long study and debate I finally surrendered one that bore the ugly visage of Chief Crazy Horse, and he wound up plumb in the center of one of the pillows.

While the dressmaker was at Grandma's the old lady never read in the evenings. There was so much news to pick up from Miss 'Mandy, so much to learn of what had happened around the county since her last visit, that Grandma put the romances away for the duration.

Grandpa and I looked forward to Miss 'Mandy's somewhat scattered appearances. It meant fancier dishes, more unusual desserts and a festive time in general. We both knew Grandma would outdo herself so that the dressmaker could carry the tidings along that Grandma was an extraordinarily fine cook—something all Windham County knew already.

Chapter 8

Maybaskets and Old Lace

MAYTIME in Windham County was a wondrous thing to behold. Grandma's great French lilac bush burst into blossom, filling the air for hundreds of yards around with its heady, overpowering scent. The johnny-jump-ups bloomed under the strawberry shrub and forsythia, and the bare spots in the front and side yards disappeared into a thick carpet of green.

Grandpa thought October with its crisp, cool air, its rich harvests, and its promise of easier days after the summer's labor in the hot fields was the best time of the whole year. But not Grandma.

"Anticipation is more exciting than consummation," she used to say. "I'll take May with its budding trees, the birds starting housekeeping and the warmth that comes after the winter."

In our town May ushered in an old tradition for the young in years, and the young in heart—the hanging of May baskets.

No one knew much about its origins, or cared, but a boy would have died of shame if he hadn't been ready on the evening of the first day of the month with a small basket, full of wild flowers, to hang on the door of his current flame—aged anywhere from ten to fourteen years.

The technique never varied to speak of. The basket was filled with damp moss, the flowers placed prettily on top with stems in the moss so they wouldn't wilt and the approach of darkness awaited with trembling and anticipation.

When it was so dark there was little fear of discovery, the boy set out from home and headed for the dwelling of his current inamorata. There he hid in the shrubbery or under a tree until he had assured himself no one was around to see him. On tip-toe he made his way up on the porch, hung the basket on the doorknob, pulled the door knocker or rapped on the glass, and then flung himself back into the shadows.

It was great fun to see the girl with the blond curls or the dark tresses open the door, look about in surprise when she found no one there, and then to witness the discovery of the love token.

Toward the end of the month the surprise element was worn very thin, and a girl had to be a fine actress to simulate consternation at discovering no caller.

If the affectionate regard for the young lady was reciprocated the boy could expect to hear a thumping on his own door and the sound of light footsteps scurrying to sanctity in the bushes beyond the steps.

Along about the middle of the month the baskets became a bit familiar to all hands concerned except that Grandma was a wonderful one to lend aid to the young man who lived at her house. She used to take scraps of velvet and put them together over old match boxes (the five-cent size) to make beautiful containers for the violets, anemones, forget-me-nots and other wild flowers.

Sometimes she made baskets out of birch bark, peeled carefully from the wood in the stove-box before she tossed it into the kitchen range. She always had bits of old lace or ribbon with which to fashion a handle, and it was rare indeed when money had to be paid out for a commercial basket. Yet no one in all of Windham County hung a prettier offering on a girl's door than the little boy who lived at Grandma's house.

This custom died out somewhere along the way when world wars, automobiles and electric porch lights that could be flashed on with a flick of the finger changed the pattern of life. Other customs came in, but they were no better, and most of them were far worse.

Maytime was also a time of mass sorrow—or it was on May 30, at least. That was the day when the soldiers' graves were decorated with flowers by little hands that had never known the faintest contact with the rigors of war.

On the 29th of May school let out at noon. Boys and girls hurried home for dinner, wolfed down their food, and then reassembled in old clothes at the schoolhouse. The school teacher, who wasn't allowed the luxury of changing into less presentable clothing, counted noses to see there were no slackers, and then led the way into the fields in search of wild flowers.

It was a strange expedition in many ways. The May baskets had denuded many a meadow of most of its blossoms, and even some of the darker glades in the woods had but few flowers left. But patriotism was a matter of burning devotion in those days and pickers never came in until they had found virtually every blossom for miles around.

All that night, until well after normal bedtime, strawberry baskets lined with tinfoil or colored paper were filled with the blooms and placed in a cool place to await the holiday on the morrow.

Grandma thought nothing of plucking the flowers from her rarest shrubs if any of our baskets looked wan and under-nourished. One way or another we saw to it that they looked as fresh as if they had come from a florist's shop.

By ten o'clock on Memorial Day morning the school children were lined up under the great arched elms along the street between the general store and the Central Vermont Station, even though everyone knew it might be an hour or more be-fore the parade from Willimantic reached our town. It wasn't easy to keep dresses and Sunday suits clean for such a long spell, but the teachers and parents managed it with a mixture of stiff discipline and appeals to our patriotism.

Just when everyone was so restless it seemed all order would be lost, the strains of band music came from the camp meet-ing road, and finally down the dusty street came the paraders from the county seat. As the bands and marchers paced by, we joined at the tag end, and without any further delay the con-tingents went on across the tracks, over the covered bridge and so to the cemetery.

It was a beautiful graveyard, with great elms towering over the mossy headstones and willows along the side nearest the river. At the end nearest the road the stones bore the names of men who died fighting under Washington, Putnam, Greene and other leaders who made the colonies free.

There were others, not so old and not so hard to decipher, that stood above the graves of other soldiers who had died in the War of 1812, the Civil War and the Spanish-American War.

At each grave a boy or girl was assigned so that no hero's resting place would go unmarked on this day of sorrow. They stood, holding their baskets of flowers, as a preacher prayed and as some local politician talked much too long and much too poorly. When the speaking was done at last, a trumpeter, carrying his bugle tied with a black ribbon, walked slowly across the graveyard to the far side, away from the people.

When he put the instrument to his lips and sounded the haunting notes of Taps each little boy and girl placed his basket on the grave of a soldier who had died to keep Windham County free and safe.

We didn't have to walk back from the cemetery. Grandpa's Stanley Steamer was the only car that could go as slowly as men walk and not stall, so the Grand Marshal let him drive right behind the band. When we cut off at the corner of the Kick Hill road, our ears rang with the noise of the brass horns and the drums, and a small boy could be forgiven if by then sorrow had given place to a rowdy sort of excitement.

So although May went out on a rather lugubrious note for Grandma, she still thought it the best month of the whole year. There was only one fly in the ointment so far as she was concerned. May was the month that Charley Overcoats reappeared and Charley made Grandma so mad you could almost see the blue flames dancing round about her.

Charley was a tramp. He was so old no one knew where he was born or where he came from. What he did in the winter was a mystery. If he possessed a last name it was lost somewhere in the musty archives. He got the name Overcoats from his habit of wearing two or three of the garments, one on top of the other, no matter what the weather. In July and August, when the temperatures on the dusty country roads were flirting with 90 and 95 and the chickens in the barnyard huddled miserably in the shade, beaks open, and panting, Charley would appear all bundled up as if for a blizzard, trudging up hill and down dale, carrying a wooden staff with a sharp nail in one end, to keep the dogs at a safe distance.

The village boys kept away too, but they watched him on his rounds as if he were a spy from another planet.

Charley was an epicure at heart, with the yearnings of a gourmet hidden within his breast under the great pile of heavy coats, so he had come to learn which farmhouses contained good cooks. He walked disdainfully past most of the places along his route. At other farms he turned down the lane and appeared at the back door to pound impatiently with his staff.

He never passed by Grandma's house.

The old lady didn't mind Charley's begging for a handout of food. As a matter of fact, she felt sorry for the old codger and kept a plate, a cup and some old cutlery on a shelf under the pump in the sink room just for the tramp. She'd heap the plate high with whatever was on the stove and brewed him tea if there was none in the pot. He ate outdoors, sitting on the back steps, glowering at the food as if each bite had been dipped in potassium cyanide. Even this ungrateful behavior didn't bother the old lady too much. But when she passed out a piece of cake for his dessert and saw him carefully pick off all the frosting and throw it away, her blood pressure shot up like steam in a tea kettle.

It was no use lecturing him. He answered her in grunts, or didn't answer at all. After he'd gone, Grandma dumped the utensils into a bucket of water in which liberal amounts of ammonia had been added. After they'd soaked for several hours she dried them in the hot sun and put them away for the next visit.

Once I asked her why she didn't wash them with the other dishes. She turned around and looked at me as if I were the only boy in all Windham County without a single brain in his head.

"How do I know he doesn't have the bad disease?" she asked. There was no other explanation offered.

Charley Overcoats followed the same route on his wanderings year after year. The section of it we knew about started down around Norwichtown. From there he plodded his lonely way to Baltic, North Franklin, Scotland, Windham Center and then on our road up over Kick Hill to Lebanon Green. Beyond that he headed toward Gardner's Lake and we lost touch with him until he came back again to Norwichtown.

He made the circuit about every four weeks in the summer, sleeping in barns and church carriage sheds. We knew when he was coming because the dogs set up a great barking when they caught his scent. The hounds and collies and other dogs ushered him from village to village, but his stick with its threatening spike made them keep their distance.

To a boy who thought the frosting on a piece of cake worth wading through a whole plate of vegetables to enjoy, there was something sacrilegious about Charley's aversion to the delicacy. He probably had cavities in his teeth and was afraid of the sugar, but to Grandma it seemed like plain cussedness.

There were times when she could have handed him a piece of plain cake, or a slice of pie, but she wouldn't give in. Charley got cake with frosting on it every time—but he was just as stubborn as Grandma. Never once did he eat it.

Chapter 9

Grandma Outfoxes the Gypsies

IT was almost as regular as clockwork. Every summer, when the ruts of late spring had been ironed out of the dirt roads of Windham County, the gypsies came to our town on their way out of nowhere to the same strange destination.

They usually arrived just as the whippoorwills began their evensong. There would be the sound of wagons creaking, harness hardware jingling, and strange, romantic voices. Then up the Norwich road would come the caravan.

Big, powerful horses pulled the heavy wagons, some covered with canvas and others built of wooden siding and roofs. From the rear doors of the latter and the tail gates of the lighter vehicles clung swarms of black-eyed children, while their mothers and fathers rode the high seat in front.

I can still recall how soon the grapevine telegraph that only small boys can operate spread the news from Kick Hill to Pigeon Swamp; from the livery stable to the crossroads store. Long before the lead horses turned up into the field behind the ball-lot every boy and girl who could crawl or walk was there to watch the gypsies bivouac.

The Yankees in our town, in whom the Puritan strain was still a tangible vein of iron, seemed to like the gypsies, if only because they represented all the freedom and license and gaiety that hard toil and bitter climate had wrung from the bodies and souls of New Englanders.

The Romany campfires were straight out of fiction to boys and girls who had to help with the chores, weed in the summer sun, carry wood in the winter, and always toe the line in austere God-fearing fashion. The gay costumes, flashy jewelry and merry songs were irresistibly appealing compared to the restricted life, the staid woolens and ginghams, and the long hours of work in Windham County.

Movies were still flickering novelties, poorly filmed and poorly directed. Radio and television were unheard of and community life was strictly limited in its horizons in those days. To a small hill town in Connecticut the gypsies came like strange characters out of adventure books—almost like people from another world. They had time for love and laughter and for song.

They represented a challenge, too. We considered it a sort of game to see if we could move about among the open fires and the parked wagons, watching the women cook and the men fiddling on violins or strumming guitars, without having

our pockets picked by the gypsy children. Many a time a favorite
jackknife or other boyish treasure disappeared, no matter how
carefully the owner tried to guard his possessions.

The town constable kept a weather eye on the nomads, but
unless they tried to get away with cattle or horses, he seldom
interfered, knowing they would be gone the next morning or, at
most, the one after that.

Grandma took a more jaundiced view of things than the
village's one peace officer. The minute the old lady learned
the gypsies had come to town she took in the washing from
the line, the porch furniture, and anything else that could be
moved without a steam shovel. Then she tied old Shep, the
collie dog, to a long rope fastened to the Rose of China tree
in the front yard.

"They'll steal the shingles off the roof if you don't look
sharp," she warned.

I used to wonder, though, whether Grandma's dislike for
the gay wanderers didn't arise from two things—an envy of the
easy manner in which the gypsy women behaved, and the
utterly wonderful aromas that drifted from the iron kettles
hung over the open campfires.

She couldn't do anything about the dark-eyed, free-striding,
high-chested women—except ignore them. But when the
gypsies were encamped nearby the old lady used to fix meals
that were unusual even for her, topped off with wondrous desserts, as if to show Grandpa and me that cooking was one field
where she'd never be content in second place.

Her old, dog-eared, battered cookbook lists many of these
recipes. One was for what she called Connecticut Beefsteak Pie.

She took three pounds of lean rump steak cut an inch thick
and then sliced it into strips three inches long and an inch
wide. The meat was "put to stew" in enough boiling water to

nearly cover it. It was allowed to simmer for a half hour. Then Grandma added a tablespoon of parsley, chopped fine, a teaspoon of thyme, a sprinkling of black pepper, a cup of sliced onions and let it stew until the meat was perfectly tender.

Next she took out a little of the liquid, rubbed into it a tablespoon of cornstarch until it had the consistency of cream, added a pinch of salt and a teaspoon of Worcestershire sauce.

Grandma put the meat in a deep pudding dish, covered it with the gravy, added grated nutmeg and baked it for a half hour.

The gypsies didn't have ovens, but even if they had had, they couldn't have turned out a more succulent dish.

Looking back at it from this considerable distance, I don't think the gypsies minded not having ovens. They had a strong preference for meat and with the help of deep iron pots suspended over the open fires, or long skewers on which they braised lamb and beef over red-hot embers, they made out very well.

We used to wonder how it was that the Romany wanderers seemed to have chicken so often when there was no evidence that they carried any with them in their big wagons. Then one night we caught a couple of the older boys raiding the chicken coops behind the Widow Martin's. They took off at a dead run and we couldn't catch them, but we found where they had lost their stolen fowl, one by one, through a hole in the bottom of their burlap sack.

If Grandma felt secure in her sturdy, well-built farmhouse, the gypsies seemed no less content in their big, gaily painted vans. The wagons, some of them obviously very old, had been embellished with art work, and some of them had tail gates and side screens done in hand-carved spindle-work. Wagon wheels and spokes were artfully painted with fine striping and even the caravan steps, which each van carried suspended under the tail gate, were carved fancifully and painted in warm colors.

Gypsies and colors went together. The women and girls wore great full skirts, most of them in gay stripes, and embroidered blouses. Even brighter colored kerchiefs were worn on their heads to keep their raven black hair in place, and every female in the camp over three years of age had earrings, bracelets and rings on.

Grandma thought they looked "a fright" and wondered how they bathed when their vans had no toilet facilities. She watched the women walking and dancing in a way no Yankee girl walked or danced, and she was convinced the Devil himself was picking out the tunes on the fiddles, mandolins and tambourines. Some of the village's gayer young men let the gypsy women read their fortunes by looking at the lines of their hands.

The old lady pooh-poohed this, allowing that the men just wanted to have their hands held by the girls with the big flashing eyes.

She didn't have to worry about Grandpa. Canny old fellow that he was, he visited the Romany camp one evening, taking his grandson with him, but leaving his big hunting-case watch, his wallet, even his small change home on the bureau. If any of the little gypsy boys were tricky enough to slip their hands in his pockets, they never found even an old jackknife.

Grandma held her pocketbook in the clutch of grim death and I doubt that six gypsies could have taken it away from her.

We younger Yankees always hated to see the gypsies move on. We went each morning to see if they were still there, and so were always on hand when the Romany men hitched up the horses to the vans, loaded the pots and other gear into the wagons, and went jingling away down the dusty road on their way to far places, taking a little romance out of life along with them.

Grandpa and I both had to admit that Grandma could cook rings around the dark-eyed, tanned and bejeweled women in the camp but we also secretly admitted that when the gypsy strangers were bivouacked in town our hearts ran a little faster and our blood pumped a little more erratically, perhaps even a little hotter.

Chapter 10

Have Another Helping

THE Congregational Church in our town sat back from the road, surrounded by a large lawn, well mowed and neat, and shaded by a row of ancient elms. No one gave the lawn much thought, except for the boys who had to keep it cut all through the summer as part of their religious training. At least they didn't give it much thought until strawberries started to ripen. Then everyone was tickled to death that we had such a fine place for a strawberry festival.

Just before the vines started bearing, the preacher would talk things over with the ladies of the Sewing Circle and out of the conference would come plans for the outdoor supper. All the parson had to do was set the date and sit back, taking it easy, because it was the women who did the cooking and the fixin'.

On the morning of the festival, some weeks later, every berry in town that was rich, ripe, red and ready was picked, stemmed and washed, packed in baskets lined with clean grape leaves and taken to the crossroads store. There the storekeeper put them in his big icebox to chill them and keep them at their peak for the evening festival. That should have been sufficient contribution on his part, but we Yankees thought no one ought to get off scot free when it came to raising funds for the Lord's work, so he had to buy dinner tickets just as all the people did who supplied the berries, baked the cakes and cookies, trimmed the tables and did all the other work.

More often than not Grandma was head of the committee on arrangements. Not only was she the best cook in the county, but she had a way of getting along with all the other women that didn't lead to ruffled feelings or tears just before time to ring the dinner bell.

After she'd sent all of her strawberries off to the store she started whipping up something for an easy noonday meal. We didn't eat fancy at noontime on a day when we knew we'd be having supper down at the church.

Being a good planner and having had plenty of experience in her long life, the old lady saved herself a lot of extra work by preparing a big pot of soup the day before such a holiday. Sometimes it would be vegetable, and other times green pea or Scotch broth, but whatever it was she'd put the pot on the stove while busy with other chores, and by the time Grandpa came in from the fields or the barn everything was well in hand.

At other times she collected leftover bits from earlier meals and put them in the center of the table, buffet style, and we took whatever struck our fancy. She often cut up day-old cake and served it with custard sauce or boiled custard. This dish she called "Traipsin' round the kitchen," speaking a bit scornfully of such rough-and-ready methods of preparing a meal.

But she always had bread and cookies and a pudding or two on hand so no one ever ran any danger of starving, even if she didn't prepare a big main course.

No one was ever known to go hungry at Grandma's, nor was it ever necessary to make a flying trip to the store.

After the midday meal the old lady changed from her dark figured calico work dress into a fancier skirt and ruffled white shirtwaist and hurried off to the church to help get ready for the supper.

"Come along," she said, "you'll be mighty handy stringing up the lanterns and running errands."

I wasn't the only boy ordered to make an appearance. By mid-afternoon most of the youngsters in the big room at grammar school (which included all grades from the fifth to the eighth) were shinnying up the elm trees, running ropes from one to the other and back and forth to the church, and tying Chinese lanterns at regular intervals to the lines.

We carried saw horses and table boards up from the basement under the Sunday school wing and set them up so the women could spread cloths over them just before time for dinner to start. They didn't dare put them on too early, what with the English sparrows that nested in the belfry.

The closer it got to the time for the guests to arrive, the more excited everyone became. The women took turns hurrying home to get dressed so there'd always be some on hand to watch the food, brew the coffee, squeeze the lemons for the lemonade and do all the other chores that had to be done to make a church supper a real success.

Grandpa drove down in the carriage, took Grandma home, and brought her right back, resplendent in a sprigged dimity dress, with a big cameo at the throat and small opal earrings.

Grandpa had his second best suit on, a black string tie, and his Congress boots polished so highly they reflected the white boiled shirt above them each time he took a step. Mr. Bacon, the storekeeper, looking just as spruce, brought the berries over in the delivery wagon and unloaded them at the back door of the Sunday school. Eager hands seized them and transferred them to big bowls and platters or crushed some to be spread on the hot shortcake.

It was turning dark by now and we used a stepladder to light the candles in the Chinese lanterns. By the time the guests started driving up, the bright light from the gay paper lamps shone down on long tables groaning under the weight of potato and vegetable salads, relishes, cold meat, fruit and mountains of strawberries. There were strawberries without trimmings, strawberries on sponge cake and on biscuit-dough shortcake, and strawberries on homemade ice cream.

Everyone seemed glad to see everyone else but they wasted no time on formalities. Families sat down around the long tables, eager to pitch into the food. No one did, though, until all the places were filled. Then the Sunday school superintendent rang the small hand bell, and the parson asked grace.

Through the years, at many a summer supper, he had learned that the congregation and the guests alike considered a long blessing something of an affront to the culinary achievements lying temptingly before their eyes.

"Dear Lord," he prayed, "we thank Thee for the opportunity

to sit down together by Thy house to partake of some of the good things that spring up under Thy ministering hand. We thank Thee also for the chance to enjoy ourselves mightily while helping with the Lord's work. Amen."

There was a ragged, but fervent, chorus of Amens, and then a great clattering and chattering as the diners tackled the job at hand.

No one held back. It was before the day when young women wanted to be so thin they wouldn't cast a shadow at high noon. Men, too, paid no mind to calories; they were even a bit eager to build up a prosperous paunch upon which to wear a heavy gold watch chain and charm. So men, women and children alike ate industriously, took second helpings and then went back for more ice cream and berries.

Usually it took two or three "sittings" to handle all the folks who drove up from far and wide, bringing good appetites as their only baggage. Those at the first serving gave up their places gladly and moved off to gossip or to take the places of the women who had drawn first duty in the kitchen.

Men sat in the wagons, conversing, or on the stone wall that ran between the churchyard and the Widow Martin's house. The children played Run-Sheepie-Run, or January, January, One, Two, Three, hollering and shouting with no thought of proper digestion. After a while it grew so dark that the only light was that from the paper lanterns swinging high over the heads of the last diners or from the lights inside the church.

That was when we shifted from the outdoor, running games to those like Spin-the-Platter or Post-Office. We cleared away the seats and benches in the Sunday school room and sat around, watching others perform, or taking our turn at enterprises that always ended up with a boy and a girl having to pay a penalty. This consisted of leaving the brightly illuminated room and going outside into the dark for a hug and a kiss before circling the church and coming back in, young faces blushing the color of field roses.

I could never justify this operation with the word "penalty" but people are slow to change, even with such things as simple terms for games.

Old Mrs. Grafton went "Tsk-tsk" at the goings-on and spoke to some of the ladies on the arrangements committee about the inordinately long time it took some of the couples to pay their penalty.

"Mercy me," retorted Grandma, hesitating not an instant, "my memory's not so short I can't remember back forty-fifty years. Seems like you always stayed out a mighty long time, and it wasn't always with Charley Grafton, either."

One night the strawberry supper ran into a bit of competition. The meal had barely started when a wagon drove by the church and came to a halt by the watering trough just outside the crossroads store. We could just make out two men fixing something, and then suddenly a kerosene oil flare was touched off, casting a bright glare over the entire vicinity. By its light we could see that it was a medicine man and his Indian Chief assistant.

The white man started to ballyhoo his product and little by little some of the men and most of the boys drifted away from the tables to listen to his spiel, and to look at a real, live "Injun."

When I got to the group of men crowded around the rear of the wagon I could see the peddler had a big row of bottles strung out along the tail gate and was offering to let us sample the contents.

It was Chief Spotted Wolf's Tonic and Pain-killer—excellent, the medicine man said positively, for summer fatigue, heat stroke, chilblains, catarrh and sounds of distant waterfalls. In Grandma's day this last was a common ailment, akin to rumblings in the head, and probably due to catarrh of the Eustachian tubes.

"Tonight we are honored to have Chief Spotted Wolf right here with us," said the peddler, as if he were introducing President McKinley himself. "The prescription for this well-nigh magic remedy for many of man's ills is known only to the Chief. I do not know what goes into each and every one of these bottles. It is the Chief's own secret, a secret handed down through generation after generation of Onondaga medicine men. I do know, however, that there is nothing in this great tonic except the roots, herbs and saps of Nature's own growing things." He paused dramatically before adding, "Plus a sufficient quantity of fine alcohol. Is that not true, Chief?"

Chief Spotted Wolf, who had been sitting on a plank behind the wagon seat, stood up majestically—every inch the noble redskin—drew his beaded and fringed robe close about him and said:

"Ugh."

"I told you so," said the peddler. "He says precious little, but every word is gospel truth."

Several of the men who had summer fatigue, or who feared the onslaught of chilblains with the coming of winter weather, paid over a dollar bill and took one of the big bottles.

For a minute it looked as if the show was over, but the peddler, smart in the ways of rural psychology, was not through by any means. He put away the unsold bottles of Chief Spotted Wolf's Tonic and Pain-killer and from under a tarpaulin cover extracted a score or more round tins, such as shoe polish is packed in. He opened one and held it up to view by the light of the flickering flare.

"Gentlemen," he said unctuously, "I am here tonight as your

true friend. You don't know me, but I am, nevertheless, your friend. I know the labors at which you toil in the fields, in the barn and in the smithy. As you work, you get dirty. It is honest dirt, but it is dirt just the same. And here I have a magic solvent that will erase, remove, take away and destroy all signs of dirt upon the skin or clothing."

He asked a boy to run to the livery stable to get a smidgin of axle grease from a wagon. Why he didn't see fit to use some from the hub of his own wagon wheel I don't know, but it was all part of his build-up. When the boy returned there was a great business of hocus-pocus as the medicine man took a handkerchief from his breast pocket, smeared it with the grease and then applied the solvent. Before our eyes there was a rubbing of hands, a fluttering of cloth, and then the handkerchief emerged as purely white as if it had just come from a laundry.

But the peddler had overstepped himself. At one side of the crowd was the Sunday school superintendent, newly arrived to see what was happening to his flock. The deacon had been around, and knew that medicine men were as smooth as pussy willows. He stood off to the side, where he was at such an angle that he saw the city slicker use sleight-of-hand to switch dirty and clean handkerchiefs. Although he was a Sunday school superintendent he was no sissy. He pointed straight at the medicine man and shouted "Fraud" in a deep bellowing voice.

Everyone looked at him. The men in the crowd started milling around as if ready to take action. Chief Spotted Wolf, who had looked all evening as if he were about to expire of extreme fatigue, leaped up, extinguished the flare with one hand and whipped the horse across the rump with the free end of the reins with the other hand. The medicine man pulled up the tail gate to save his wares, and the wagon bucketed away noisily in the pitch-black darkness.

Chapter 11

Listen for the Tin Peddler

ONE of the most powerful influences on Yankee cooking in days gone by was the tin peddler. He didn't realize it himself, but he exerted more power than he knew, carrying recipes up and down the deeply rutted roads from town to town, like a slow but honored diplomatic courier.

Back before the garage supplanted the carriage house the tin peddler visited our town in Windham County three or four times each summer. His bright red wagon, packed full of crockery, cutlery, pots and pans, and with buckets, copper boilers, skillets and roasting pans hanging between the wheels and on the tailboard, was a great institution.

Grandma cooked three meals a day, seven days a week, and the stoutest saucepans and double boilers had a way of wearing out, so she was a good customer for the itinerant salesman. Often, after making a purchase, she'd be given a note from a relative or she'd send one to my Aunt Freelove, Aunt Patience or to Uncle Welcome's wife.

Many times these messages contained recipes requested the last time the tin peddler had passed through on his rounds. Yankee thrift grabbed at the chance to send correspondence without paying for stamps.

One of the recipes that was exchanged in this way—although Grandma never would admit where it came from—was the one she used for baked cranberry beans. In our family we had no use for California pea beans, holding them fit only for chicken feed.

Grandma picked over and washed carefully a pound of the pretty beans, splotched and marked like tiny bird eggs, and then soaked them in water overnight. She used enough to keep them well covered, even after they had absorbed some and had swelled up plump and full, as they would be in six or eight hours. In the morning she parboiled them on top of the stove until the skins were just ready to crack.

With a slatted spoon she put a layer of beans in a glazed earthen bean pot, then a layer of sliced onions, salt and pepper, and a sprinkling of dark brown sugar. Sometimes she used dark molasses instead and only Grandpa could tell the difference (or at least he claimed he could tell), and the old lady was so kindhearted she never showed him up if he guessed incorrectly.

Next she cut a quarter pound of lean salt pork in half and

diced one of the halves. She continued filling the pot, layer by layer, and scattered the bits of pork throughout.

When the pot was about full she scored the remaining chunk of pork with a sharp knife and stuck it in the beans so that one corner stuck up like a small Gibraltar. Over it all went the liquor from the parboiling.

Grandma put the lid on the pot and set it in the oven which she had slowed down, and cooked it for at least six hours. Sometimes she left the lid off for the last hour or so to brown the top layer and give those beans a crunchy consistency. If the beans dried out, though, she added more liquor or warm water. In the winter she usually left them in the oven all night, but with Grandma's busy day this was seldom much longer than six or seven hours.

In Windham County very few people used ketchup on baked beans. Grandma thought it about on a par with dancing in church. With her it was chili sauce or nothing.

Her recipe for this delicacy, which came from my Aunt Annie, called for chopping up eighteen ripe tomatoes, two green peppers, and six onions. She cooked them until tender and then added a cup of sugar, two and a half cups of cider vinegar, two teaspoons of salt and one teaspoon each of cinnamon, allspice and nutmeg, and a half teaspoon of ground cloves. She cooked everything for another fifteen minutes and then canned the chili sauce, putting it away to ripen before bringing it up from the cellar whenever Saturday night rolled around.

When the snow was drifting down outside the kitchen windows and the lamps flickered in the brackets on the wall, the smell of this highly spiced chili sauce rising from a deep plate of baked cranberry beans was something to make a country boy dream of Dyak headhunters and South Sea go-downs.

We ate steamed brown bread with our beans. Nothing else

was considered quite cricket. Grandma made more than enough of everything so that the kids could have cold bean sandwiches on brown bread next day.

Nothing in the world tasted so good when a fellow was fishing for pickerel through the ice and had to keep moving to watch the tip-ups.

Another recipe that was delivered to Grandma by the tin peddler was the one for Maple Butternut Pie. There were no sugar maples on Grandpa's farm, but a big butternut tree grew not far outside the parlor windows. Each fall we gathered the nuts the squirrels hadn't made off with, and spread them on the floor of the barn loft to season for the winter's cooking. Maple sugar could be bought at the general store, and Grandma had everything else that was needed right in her own buttery.

She made the pie crust while I opened the nuts with a hammer and a flatiron, the latter utensil gripped loosely between my knees so the shocks wouldn't be so sharp. Then she mixed two cups of milk and a cup of maple sugar in a double boiler over boiling water and heated it until the sugar was dissolved. There were other ingredients—eggs, cornstarch, flavorings— and all of it joined together with much stirring and beating and blending.

By this time, if I hadn't eaten too many of them in the process of opening the shells, there would be three-fourths of a cup of butternut meats all ready. These were chopped on a wooden board, but not too fine, and stirred into the filling.

The old lady lined the pie tin with the pie crust pastry, poured in the mixture and sometimes dusted the surface with a little cinnamon and nutmeg. After it was cooked she put a meringue on top and placed it back in the oven to brown.

Butternut trees are mighty hard to find these days. Talk all you will about pecans, walnuts, and other nuts on the market today, there's none to compare with the rich, zesty meats that came from the long, dark shells of the butternuts. They made this pie something to sing praises to.

Eating a big wedge of it made you proud you were a Yankee, and prouder yet of Grandma.

Chapter 12

Grandma Loved a Parade

GRANDPA kept the Stanley Steamer in the carriage house, a building larger than most modern dwellings. It had a cupola on top, surmounted by a weather vane. The slatted sides of the cupola had become dislodged slightly so that barn swallows were able to fly in and out, tucking their wings in tight to their sides at the precise instant their trajectory took them through the cracks.

People who live on farms love swallows, knowing their insatiable appetite for large quantities of mosquitoes. But Grandma's affection for them was watered down considerably by the knowledge that the swallows, making their mud and wattle nests on the rafters, were nowhere near such neat housekeepers as she was. They dropped little bits of straw and feathers and sometimes spilled the wet mud they carried in their beaks from the always damp spillage area around the watering trough. Much of it fell on the canvas top of the automobile. Some even got inside on the tufted-leather seat cushions.

Whenever the old couple planned an outing Grandpa had to wipe and polish the car while the steam pressure built up in the boiler. One morning, not long after school was out for the summer, he was busy with whiskbroom and cloth when the old lady marched out to the carriage house like a clipper ship under a full suit of sails.

"Land sakes," she cried, "if you don't get a move on we won't get to the city before the parade's all over and done."

"Pshaw," grumbled Grandpa, "I'll bet the fire enjines ain't even left yet—and they're horse-drawn at that."

He was right. In the firehouses in Windham Center, Scotland, Westminster, Chaplin, Lebanon, Canterbury and Eagleville the volunteer firemen were still rubbing and polishing the great pumpers, sifting the coal so it wouldn't be so dusty when they stoked the fires, and wiping the harnesses with neat's-foot oil.

It was the Fourth of July and the parade was to start on the dot of noon.

But Grandma was impatient. She spent so many hours in her home, busy with cooking and cleaning and mending, that she didn't have much opportunity to be with other people. When a chance like a parade or a church supper came along she didn't want to miss a single minute of it.

She stood over us, almost pushing the breakfast down our

throats, urging us to hurry, and snatching up dishes to wash them as soon as they were no longer needed. By ten o'clock the beds had been made, the dishes done, the kitchen was spotless and the entire house dusted.

"A body can't tell," said Grandma. "Your grandfather might bring someone home with us and I'd sooner be skinned alive than have them see what a poor housekeeper I am."

Anyone could see that you could eat off the floor, it was so clean, but he'd never be able to convince the old lady.

She put the cat out, then carried a deep saucer of rich milk and cream out to the barn, putting it in the manger of a stall used only for visitors' horses. On the way back past the woodpile she picked up the handaxe and split several pieces of white birch, taking them into the kitchen and dumping them into the wood box. Chopping wood held a strange fascination for Grandma. Grandpa kept the wood box piled high, and plenty of small kindling in the chip basket under the stove, yet the old lady never went out to the barn without stopping on the way back to split a few pieces. Her eye was as true and her hand as steady as they were the day she was married, way back before the Blizzard of '88.

White birch is wonderful wood for a stove, most of it so straight-grained a single stroke with a sharp blade will rive it as easily as though it were held together with nothing but egg white.

This morning, eager as she was to get to the city to see the Independence Day parade, she couldn't forego the little pleasure of wielding the axe on the birch a couple of times.

She made up for the delay by a great bustling and hustling, and long before the old clock on the mantel tapped its one note for ten-thirty o'clock we were all in the Stanley Steamer, headed for Willimantic. Streaming out from behind what was then called the tonneau was a fine plume of steam, just enough to avoid an explosion but not enough to bleed off the pressure.

Grandpa tooled the car past the fire engine from Scotland before we reached the Methodist Camp Meeting grounds; and when we shot by the great La France engine from South Windham, with four matched grays pulling eagerly against their collars, Grandma began to breathe a little easier.

Even in those days parking on a holiday was no easy matter. All along Main Street there were rigs and buggies and surreys standing at the curbs, the horses securely tied to telephone poles or with hitching weights fastened to their bits. Here and there one could see an occasional Buick, Stevens-Duryea or Loco-mobile, looking out-of-place and strange among the horse-drawn vehicles.

Grandpa drove around a block and stopped on a side street right at the intersection of Main Street, headed so that we could see everything as well as though we were in a reviewing stand.

He took off his great leather gauntlets, pulled out his big gold watch and held it under Grandma's nose.

"Not even eleven o'clock yet," he grumbled, "and nothing due to start until noon."

"Mercy," said Grandma, happy as a lark to be where she could see so many people, "you're as cross as two sticks. I'll bet you're hungry."

She took off her linen duster and veil—the sun by now was beating down mercilessly, sparkling and glinting on the brightly polished brass headlights, windshield frame and hard-ware—reached into the tonneau, and brought forth a lunch basket.

Inside, under layers of white napkins and dampened cloths, there were ham sandwiches, slices of mocha cake, big red apples and jars of cold tea, wrapped in wet newspapers to stay cool. Grandpa preferred egg-salad or chicken sandwiches because they were easier to chew with his store teeth, but the old lady didn't trust the hot weather, fearing such foods would spoil too easily.

We ate in style, watching the band players going by to the assembly point, and chatting with friends the old couple hadn't seen since the last Grange meeting or the Memorial Day ceremonies at the cemetery. There were Mr. and Mrs. Pearsall, who ran the creamery in Lebanon; old Doctor Williams from Scotland; and the Wheelers from over the ridge in North Franklin. Mrs. Pearsall and Grandma had grown up together, gone to school, church and barn dances together, learned to paint china together and got married within a few months of each other.

They talked and laughed as though they were back in "Professor" Blake's geography class, although the school teacher had been dead at least forty years. To a small boy, who would have preferred to be playing on the courthouse steps, or racing in and out among the horses and carriages with the other boys, it sounded a little silly, but then, most of the stuff women talked about was so much nonsense. They wouldn't have known whether Tris Speaker and Bullet Joe Wood were ball players or trotting horses, and wouldn't have cared a tittle.

The leather seats got so hot they felt like stove lids when anyone shifted his position. Grandpa was wilting under his cap, coat, stiff collar, bow tie, and starched shirt, but Grandma somehow managed to look as cool as a watermelon that had been left overnight in a bucket lowered in the well. She never used any makeup—paint and powder were only for "fancy ladies"—but she had rubbed her cheeks with her hairbrush before leaving the farm and they still looked as fresh and rosy as a young girl's.

The last glass of tea had just been finished off when the clock in the courthouse dome boomed twelve o'clock. Way down where the New Haven tracks to Providence cut across lower Main Street there was a loud crash from the ancient gun captured by the Eleventh Connecticut Infantry at Antietam, and the parade got under way.

Old Colonel Lathrop J. Weatherbee, who had fought under Meade at Gettysburg, led the marchers, mounted on a great chestnut gelding. He had accumulated so many medals from Grand Army of the Republic encampments that he listed a bit to port, looking like the president of a Banana Republic.

Behind the Colonel rode all the politicians who dared straddle a horse in public, and then came the Fife and Drum Corps of the Putnam Phalanx, a company of the Governor's Foot Guard, and a detachment of Spanish-American War veterans.

It was hotter than the middle grate of a blast furnace and everyone's uniform was cut out of heavy woolen cloth, it being well before the day of summer khaki or tropical worsteds. Grandpa was wilting fast, but Grandma was enjoying herself so much she forgot to be warm.

After the heroes of Windham County had passed, the fire companies rolled by, each one with a great steam pumper drawn by four or six stout horses. The fire engines were burnished and bright and every harness was polished until it looked as if it had been lacquered. There were fires under each boiler, and the engineers riding the platform at the rear of each vehicle were kept jumping as they fed the fiery-red maws of the fireboxes and tinkered with valves to keep everything from blowing up smack in the middle of Main Street.

"Creation," exploded Grandma, "I can't for the life of me see why they have to have fires in 'em on the Fourth of July."

Grandpa looked at her pityingly.

"You think those boys are going to practice and polish all year and run to fires in the middle of the night," he asked, "and not have sparks flying outen the stacks when they parade?"

When the company from South Windham rolled by, the old lady stood up and waved vigorously. The chief, riding high above the rumps of the nigh span, rose to his feet and made as pretty a bow in Grandma's direction as he could manage without pitching out onto the cobblestone pavement.

She applauded the other companies politely but showed them no special favor. As a matter of fact, when a few visiting outfits that had no big pumpers marched by, pulling hose carts, the old lady even went so far as to withhold approval.

She sat patiently while the Camp Fire Girls and the high school bands marched by, but when the tail end of the parade began to grow a little rag-tailed and shabby—as most parades have a way of doing—Grandma suggested we all have a glass of Moxie; and we climbed out of the Stanley Steamer and hurried into the dark, relatively cool interior of a drug store.

In those days ladies didn't sit on the stools at the "sody fountain." Grandma dropped into a chair at a small round table, arranged her skirts to make room for our legs, and sat regally by as the clerk mixed the syrup and carbonated water at the ornate marble fountain.

There was never a day when her husband worked in the hot fields that the old lady didn't fix a cooling drink for him, and we were used to shrubs, cold cider and lemonade. But this was something else again. The Moxie bubbled in the glasses in such a way that a small boy could hardly keep from sneezing, something lemonade never did. And there was something genteel about using a paraffin paper straw that set the whole operation on a very high level.

We drove back to the farm, very hot but very happy. On the

way we passed by Silas Black's place and saw where the chicken house had burned down after being struck by lightning in a sudden storm that hadn't caused even a drop of rain to fall on the parade, a few short miles away. The embers were still smoking and Silas was standing by, dejectedly, with buckets of water handy, to keep the fire from blowing up and spreading to other buildings.

"That's it," said the old lady, "the fire engine gets taken off to the city and a man's place burns mighty nigh down."

Grandpa never took his eyes off the ruts in the dusty road.

"A few boards and some wire and Silas will have himself a new chicken house," he said testily. "Mebbe it'll learn him to take out insurance on his house and barn, the old skinflint."

As soon as the car had been run into the carriage house, with valves and petcocks turned off carefully, Grandpa changed into overalls for the evening chores, and Grandma took off her fancy things and put on calico and a gingham apron.

The old man stopped at the door, took a comb from a wall bracket, and ran it through his thick thatch of snow-white hair. It was an aluminum comb that bore the words "Electro-magnetic hair saver" engraved on it. A dozen world-famous scientists couldn't have convinced him that it wasn't exactly as advertised.

Chapter 13

Raspberry Shrub and Mulled Cider

THE Central Vermont Railroad ran through Windham County on its way to the sea at New London. Once, years ago, there had been a grandiose dream that it would give the Canadian National line a warm-weather outlet, an ice-free port that could substitute for Montreal and Halifax. The vision withered, however, like the Russian Czar's dream of a warm-seas harbor in the south.

Before the automobile disrupted things, the CV handled a lot of freight and operated several passenger trains, but the change was already apparent to the trained eye. Business was falling off even before Grandma admitted it. The younger generation knew what was happening, though.

On hot, sultry days in midsummer the kids used to walk barefooted down to the station to watch the infrequent trains rumble by. The fascination of far places was more tangible there, with the different names on the boxcars hinting at distant cities and states.

No one wore shoes from the Fourth of July to Labor Day, except on Sunday, and then only under noisy protest. By late August and September the bottoms of the boys' feet were so tough they could stand almost anything. That was another reason why the railroad station was such a lure. By late afternoon the tracks were quivering with heat and it took all the nerve a boy could muster to walk barefoot along the steel strips from the freight house to the bridge over the Shetucket River.

After such a test of stout-hearted courage there was no delight equal to sipping a tall glass of Raspberry Shrub, which Grandma always kept on hand in the root cellar.

Grandma used either the redcaps or the blackcaps, depending on her whim at the time she prepared the concoction, but she always contended that the redcaps made the drink a little more tangy.

In New England folks used what they had and made it do, but they were so clever about it no one ever wanted for anything. We hardly knew what soda pop was. Once in a while, when we went to the fair, or to see the firemen parade on the Fourth of July, the old lady would splurge and we'd have a glass of Moxie apiece. Such an event made it a red-letter day, but the Raspberry Shrub would have tasted just as good if it had come in a bottle.

When the berries were at their peak of ripeness, and the catbirds were starting to raid the berry patch, we picked as many as we could to save the crop. It was no fun, what with the briars and the nasty chiggers that burrowed into your skin and turned ankles and legs into small, but fiery, lava patches.

Grandma sorted and picked over carefully four quarts of the fruit, placing the berries in a large glazed earthenware crock. Then she poured one and a half pints of cider vinegar over them and let them stand for three days in a cool place.

On the fourth day she strained the mixture through a flannel bag, squeezing the cloth a little but not enough to force any of the pulp through. Adding two cups of sugar for each pint of juice, she boiled it briskly for fifteen minutes in an enamel saucepan. Only Grandma always called it graniteware.

When it was cooled, she poured it into bottles, corked them tightly and set them in the root cellar. Then when small boys came home, hot and thirsty from walking the hot tracks or playing one-old-cat, Grandma would send them for the "makings," pour three tablespoons of the juice into a glass of the coldest water, and serve it with sugar cookies.

I can still remember that Grandpa had a way of appearing precisely at the instant the Raspberry Shrub was poured. He could sense what Grandma was doing, whether he was in the hayloft or the milk shed.

On the kitchen wall Grandma had a calendar with big pages and it was always covered with scribblings. That's how she kept track of all her long-term food preparations, egg money, tax-paying days, births, marriages and other vital events in the village. Each morning she glanced at it as a bank president does at his desk pad. On the right days she did the right things, and so never had any trouble, no matter how involved the recipe was.

There was another quick thirst quencher Grandma used to whip up if she happened to be out of other "makings," or if she was too busy to spend much time. She called it Cream-of-tartar Water. That was all there was to it, really. The old lady didn't have a very high regard for baking powder in her younger days, using baking soda and cream-of-tartar instead. As she grew older and things were modernized, Grandma changed a little too, and took to using baking powder, although there were some things, like light cakes, and delicate items of that sort, which she still made with the two separate ingredients. So she always had cream-of-tartar on hand. For the drink she put a little bit of powder into a glass of cold water, flicked in a little brown sugar, and stirred it well. To a thirsty boy it wasn't half bad.

When the days grew shorter and the evenings chilly, Grandma had another drink appropriate to the season and the weather. This was mulled grape juice, a delicacy that a boy could enjoy just before lighting the kerosene lamp and going upstairs to bed.

There was no heat in the bedrooms and the warmth generated by the mulled grape juice lasted until the sheets lost most of their icy coldness.

I can still see Grandma getting this drink ready on the big range in the kitchen. She mixed two cups of grape juice, a cup of sugar and a cup of water in a deep pan. She tied a stick of cinnamon, broken into small pieces, and six whole cloves into a little cloth sack; tossed it into the liquid and brought the mixture just to a boil.

The old lady stirred it for ten minutes over the low heat at the back of the stove, timing herself by the ancient clock on the mantel. Then she removed the spice bag, squeezed in the juice of a lemon, and served it piping hot, using an earthenware teapot.

Naturally, Grandma made her own grape juice from rich, tangy Concord grapes that grew along the arbor leading to the milk house. It was my job, however, to hike up into the woods after the first frost and gather some wild fox-grapes, so that the juice would have the added zest Grandma demanded.

When the evenings were raw and windy and the mulled juice was served from the old teapot, it made you glad you had scouted successfully for the wild grapes and found them before the thieving bluejays had stripped the vines.

Grandpa preferred mulled cider to the hot grape juice. It was even easier to prepare. While he was mending harness, whittling new rungs for the chair he was always wearing out by tilting it back against the wall and catching his heels on them, or doing other inside jobs, Grandma fixed the cider.

She put a quart of cider, five whole cloves, three whole all-spice and a two-inch stick of cinnamon into a saucepan together. She cooked it over very low heat for fifteen minutes, stirring it all the time. Then she strained it through a cloth and served it hot.

Grandpa could make a mug of it last through the reading of a whole issue of the *Farm Journal* or *The Rural New Yorker.* The old man took a lot of kidding down at the general store and post office about subscribing to *The Rural New Yorker,* but it was surprising how often some of his neighbors would ask to borrow it when he was done reading—and every one of them a Connecticut man, born and bred.

"My father had to go over into Rhode Island to get a wife," he used to say at such times. "Why shouldn't I read a magazine from York State?"

Chapter 14

Picnicking with a Stanley Steamer

IT was early on Saturday morning that Grandma started to get ready to go riding Sunday afternoon. Many's the time she barely made it. The old lady loved to go adventuring in Grandpa's Stanley Steamer.

The process went about like this: After the weekend's baking had been set on the shelves to cool and the cinnamon doughnuts cached away in the stone crock, Grandma went to the telephone on the kitchen wall and gave the handle a few brisk whirls.

Usually nothing happened until the old lady had rung ten or fifteen minutes. Then the operator—Mrs. Parker—came up out of the cellar, or in from the garden, and asked whom Grandma wanted to talk to. Nobody used numbers; life was a lot more personal then.

Grandma and the operator, who had the small switchboard in her sitting room, talked about the church social, the weather, Mrs. Parker's catarrh, and divers other subjects until the old lady was about ready to hang up, thinking she'd had a long enough conversation.

"Land sakes alive," she'd say, "I almost forgot. Get me Nettie on the wire."

Nettie was her niece, who lived across from the general store down at the village crossroads.

After talking to Nettie and inviting her to go on the ride, Grandma hung up and started to get food together so that no one would starve on the thirty- or forty-mile ride the next day. You'd have thought the couple were planning a trip to the Yukon.

The next morning while Grandma packed a wicker picnic basket, Grandpa went out to the barn—he never did learn to call it the garage—and played a flame from a blow torch on the pilot of the car's boiler. Half an hour later, with the turning of scores of valves and the taking of pressure readings from as many gauges, the old gentleman had enough steam up to start off.

But he didn't go anywhere then. Heck no. He was still in overalls. So he had to go in and wash up, put on a clean shirt with a hard collar, a bow tie, a good suit, a cap, a linen duster and goggles. By then Grandma too was ready, and so was Nettie and so was I. Everyone had on a linen duster except me. Small boys were expected to get dirty.

We started off down the dirt road with a plume of steam issuing from behind the tonneau, as we called it, and half the horses we passed stood up on their hind legs and snorted. The other half laid their ears back along their heads and bared their teeth.

Because they had no condensers, those early Stanleys lost so much water that before we got to Norwichtown we had to take on a new supply. Grandpa pulled up alongside the nearest horse trough, threw a hose in and siphoned several gallons into the reservoir tank.

The loafers gawked at this and Grandpa got a big kick out of telling them he used water for fuel, which made the Stanley Steamer the cheapest car on the road to operate.

If there were no flat tires to be patched and pumped up we used to leave the highway, drive down a lane somewhere into a field, and eat the picnic lunch Grandma had prepared.

There was fried chicken along with ham sandwiches between slices of homemade bread and other stout gastronomic supplies. And always there were Banbury Tarts and Raisin Drop Cookies.

Grandma made her pastry in the usual way (see page 165) and cut it into three-inch squares. The filling was made by cooking a half cup each of raisins, currants, and figs, all chopped fine, with two tablespoons of water in a double boiler for twenty minutes. Then four tablespoons of orange or lemon juice were added; a cup of sugar and two teaspoons of flour, mixed well, were put in next and the mixture cooked for twenty minutes. After the filling was taken from the fire a half cup of chopped butternuts was stirred in. (A more modern recipe is shown on page 201.)

The old lady turned the corners of the pastry up and pinched them together, slit the tops and brushed them with milk. It took twenty minutes in a hot oven to turn them into a delicacy without equal.

She made the raisin cookies by adding a cup of water to two and a half cups of raisins and boiling them briskly. Then they were allowed to cool before a teaspoon of baking soda was added. Next she put in two cups of sugar and a cup of butter, well creamed together, followed by one teaspoon of vanilla and one of lemon flavoring and three well-beaten eggs.

Grandma sifted four cups of flour, a teaspoon and a half of baking powder, a half teaspoon of salt, a teaspoon of cinnamon and a fourth of a teaspoon each of nutmeg and allspice. This was stirred in and then a cup of walnuts or butternuts added.

She dropped the batter off a teaspoon onto a cooky sheet and cooked the lumps twelve to fifteen minutes in a moderately hot oven.

After they were done, they were removed at once, cooled and stored to ripen a few days in a tightly covered stone crock.

There was enough nourishment in them to help a man pump up two flat tires. But that wasn't why we ate them. We just couldn't say "No," to Grandma's raisin drops.

Chapter 15

Grandma Loved Premiums

FROM the top of the hill, on a warm summer day, you could hear the dogs bugling ten or fifteen minutes before the butcher wagon crawled up from the Pigeon Swamp Road, crested the ridge, and started down toward the village.

To Grandma, working busily in the big farm kitchen, the barking was a signal as precise as today's radio-alarm clock. She'd push the kettles back from the hot part of the wood stove, smooth her hair, take her purse from the shelf in the buttery and go out to wait for Mr. White to drive up.

The butcher wagon had a canvas top like a small prairie

80

schooner, and the whole vehicle was painted white to reflect the sun's rays and help keep the interior cool. Inside, the quarters of beef, the young spring lambs and the pork loins and hams were covered with clean cloths and nestled around a huge chunk of ice cut the winter before on the fulling-mill pond and stored in the ice house.

Grandma had been buying her meat from Mr. White since around the time of the Blizzard of '88. They were fast friends and no one ever knew them to haggle over price or quality.

Sometimes, when the last place is taken in the supermarket parking lot, or when the clerk says liver is a dollar fifty a pound, I think Grandma had all the best of it. By walking less than one hundred feet she could get any cut of meat she desired, from a prime animal butchered by an expert.

Mr. White threw in liver and kidneys free of charge, and huge marrow bones with which to make soup stock. Any customer who had a dog or cat got things like lungs and lights and scraps as a matter of course, and no one had to ask for—or pay for—suet with which to lard a roast or make a suet pudding.

Whenever the wagon stopped, all the cats and most of the dogs from roundabout appeared as though they had been called, their eyes snapping and jowls slavering. I never saw one go away without a tidbit.

Fresh meat wasn't the only thing that Grandma bought without leaving home. On Fridays a fishmonger drove up and down the country roads, heralding his coming with long blasts on a battered tin horn.

Every other week the Grand Union Tea man drove through, bringing a basket of teas, coffees, spices and flavorings to the kitchen door for Grandma's inspection. He was a great trial for the old lady because he always had "specials," such as a pound box of cinnamon and a baking dish for the price of the cinnamon, or lemon extract and a flour sifter that cost no more than the bottle of flavoring.

Once when the spice and tea peddler was pushing a new variety of vanilla Grandma bought so often and so heavily to get the special prizes that she had a half dozen large bottles of the extract on the shelf in the spice cabinet. Grandpa swore the old lady was flavoring everything with vanilla just to use it up and he hollered for lemon but it didn't do him any good. That year Grandma said "Make mine vanilla" and she made it stick.

One of her favorite dishes was a vanilla flavored concoction she called "Satin Pudding." It was as light as a spring cloud, everyone said, although I never saw anyone eat a cloud and couldn't figure out how they'd be able to make the comparison. One thing was certain. It was as smooth as a medicine man's spiel about Chief Crazy Horse's cure for the rheumatiz.

Grandma put one cup of sugar into a quart of milk and brought it almost to a boil. She dissolved three tablespoons of cornstarch in half a cup of cold milk and blended it with the well-beaten yolks of five eggs. Then she stirred this into the hot milk and cooked it until it was as thick as heavy cream.

Next the old lady removed it from the fire, added a pinch of salt and one and a half teaspoons of vanilla, mixing it all together, and poured it into a baking dish. She whipped up a meringue made of five egg whites, beaten very stiff, and with five tablespoons of sugar to flavor, and spread it over the top of the pudding. Then the dish was put in the big wood range and baked until a light brown. Grandma always served her Satin Pudding very cold, and people who ate it for the first time used to get confused, thinking they had reached heaven by a short cut.

It was the same way with her veal stew and dumplings. I've

seen tears come to the eyes of field hands who—after a big second helping—suddenly realized the dish was empty. This was Grandma's recipe:

Cut two and a half pounds of rump or shoulder of veal, boned, into two-inch pieces. Cover with one and a half quarts of water. Add a quarter cup of chopped onion, half a bay leaf, and a teaspoon of salt. Put the lid on and simmer until the meat is tender. Never let it come to a boil. Remove the piece of bay leaf, add one tablespoonful of homemade ketchup and season to taste with salt and pepper.

After the stew had seasoned for a day and a night the old lady heated it up again, made dumplings, and dropped the batter off by the tablespoonful, on top of the stew. Then she covered the pot and cooked it for fifteen minutes, never once removing the lid.

I can still see her lifting the dumplings, golden and fluffy, out of the pot with two long forks, placing them on a hot platter and putting the stew and thickened gravy over and around them.

The cat fared badly on the days Grandma made veal stew with dumplings. If it hadn't been for the butcher's tidbits she'd have had to go looking for her meal in the barn. There were never any leftovers from the stew.

Chapter 16

The Sunday School at the Seashore

ABOUT the only time Grandma ever got to see the ocean was on the annual picnic of the Congregational Church Sunday school. But she could cook fish as if she had grown up on Point Judith or Cuttyhunk Island.

The picnic may have been a holiday for the kids, but to Grandma it was a chore that started before the barn swallows came twittering out of the carriage house in the morning, and ended long after dark. On the day of the outing she arose early and packed a great wicker hamper with enough lunch to feed a battalion. Then she shepherded the young'uns into the big farm carryall and drove off to the Central Vermont Depot.

When the morning accommodation came rattling around the bend she somehow managed to keep all the children from being run over and then led them into the special car reserved for the Sunday school. Two hours later they were all at the beach.

The line between adults and children was never more sharply defined than at the beach. While the oldsters ate a shore dinner the kids ate ham and chicken sandwiches, drumsticks, and coconut cake. I never knew why the children were denied the delectable dishes fresh from the ocean, but it had something to do with a fear that strange foods and strange surroundings at the same time were deleterious to a child's welfare. Anyway it was Grandma's rule and everyone abided by it.

Yet back in Windham County, where she herself could preside over stewpan and skillet, the old lady fixed fish and chowders that must have made the angels envious.

When the shad was running in the rivers, Grandma served roe for breakfast and contended it had not only the properties of a spring tonic but was a brain food, too.

She covered the roe from one shad with water, added a teaspoon of salt and a tablespoon of vinegar, and put it on the front of the stove to boil for twenty minutes. Next the roe was drained, covered with cold water and allowed to stand for ten minutes. Once more it was drained, sprinkled with salt and pepper, and rolled in flour. Thus blanketed, it was fried in deep fat until the flour turned a light oak in color.

I have no scientific proof that the roe was a good spring tonic, and, what with one thing and another, I've come to doubt it was brain food, but it was a wonderful experience to come tumbling downstairs from the bedroom under the eaves into a kitchen redolent with the smell of golden brown shad roe.

Grandma would have had a hard time with so many hungry mouths if she hadn't served Cape Cod Turkey at least once a week. Miles Standish and Cotton Mather are no more a part of the Yankee heritage than the Gorton people in Gloucester. Somewhere in every farmhouse there was a wooden box, made to look as if tied with fishline, and rough to the touch from both splinters and dried salt crystals. Inside, the box was packed tightly with dry, salted fillets of cod.

The night before Grandma served creamed codfish, which is what "furriners" call Cape Cod Turkey, she soaked as much fish as she needed in cold water. The next morning she changed the water several times to get rid of most of the salt and then simmered it until the fish flaked.

In another pan she melted a piece of butter the size of a bantam's egg, added a teaspoon of flour, a few grains of freshly ground pepper and stirred it until it started to boil. Next she added warm milk, enough to make a sauce. Then the flaked fish and a well-beaten egg yolk were added and the mixture allowed to blend well over the slow part of the stove.

Grandma poured the creamed fish over boiled white potatoes and shook a little Hungarian paprika over it, as much to add a little color as to alter the taste.

If the whippoorwills weren't wailing—a sure sign of inauspicious events—Grandma often cooked up a pot of kedgeree for breakfast, or for a holdover supper if the men were plowing and planting late into the soft, spring evenings. The recipe came from Grandma's relatives on the eastern shore of Narragansett Bay; they had obtained it from forbears who had sailed clipper ships around the Horn and along the coasts of Ceylon and India.

It may have been good eating in the Spice Islands. In Windham County, under Grandma's loving tutelage, it was something to burn incense to.

(The ingredients are listed on page 118.)

When the rice was soft and fluffy the other ingredients were added tenderly and the whole mixture allowed to become hot in a double boiler.

Served piping hot, it was a meal that stayed the pangs of hunger with an iron hand, yet the velvet warmth of the Indies was there, and the tang of the sea as well.

Chapter 17

Grandpa's Club

EVERY Saturday evening after supper Grandpa lighted the
coal-oil lantern and walked the two miles downhill to the crossroads store. By the time he got there, six or seven other men
had gathered in the back room, where they hitched the captain's
chairs close to the pot-bellied stove and stoked up their pipes.

In our town it was the only club. On prayer meeting night
it was deserted, but at other times it hummed with talk of
politics, crops, good fishing or hunting or what to do about the
peach blight.

It was a wondrous place, to which a small boy seldom gained

access alone, and always only if he sat still and held his tongue. Along one wall were three huge wooden vats, lying on their sides. One held kerosene, one vinegar, and the third one molasses. The odors hung in a redolent suspension, each one, strangely enough, easily distinguishable.

About the only time the storekeeper could join in the conversation was when he brought in an oil can, with a raw potato jammed on the spout, to draw some oil, or earthenware demijohns for vinegar or molasses. In the winter it took so long to fill the jug with molasses he could get in quite a bit of talk before going out front again.

Along another wall were bins of seeds and barrels of crackers —milk, soda and graham. The farmers ate as many of these as they wanted, all through the evening, and left a few coins on the counter when they went home. It was a sort of honor system and no one was ever known to take advantage of the grocer.

Buckets, sections of harness, plow points, shotguns and felt boots hung from pegs on the walls or from hooks driven into the ceiling. Just inside the door from the main store room there was a rack of buggy whips—their butts bright with colored strips of leather and their tips bearing fancy tassels.

The arrangement in the main section was of necessity a little more orderly. Counters ran along both sides and part of the rear, leaving room for access to the back room. Behind the counters were shelves to the ceilings, weighted down with yard goods, groceries, hardware and notions. String hung down from metal containers resembling small bee hives, and wrapping paper was more common than bags or boxes.

On one counter was a thread cabinet, a cabinet-maker's work of art. It had a dozen drawers, all with glass fronts, and the brightly hued spools shone out like bits of stained glass in a church window.

There were only two glass-covered showcases. One held jewelry and small notions, buttons and hooks-and-eyes, and other odds and ends. The other was full of candy. There were chocolate bonbons, filled with hard creams; others with soft fondant centers; and all the varieties little boys and girls longed for when empty handed, or spent long minutes choosing when they had a penny.

There were long licorice whips, cinnamon buttons as big as a quarter, candy corn, marshmallow ears of corn, and tiny tin frying pans with candy in them resembling fried eggs. With each frying pan came an even smaller tin spoon, guaranteed to cut young tongues or lips unless handled with extreme care.

On Saturday nights the grocer roasted peanuts in a crude roaster built like an old victrola. There was a large kerosene lamp in the bottom, and where the turntable would be there were two trays with wire mesh bottoms.

Each time the storekeeper went by as he filled orders for the customers he shook the trays to roast the peanuts more evenly. By eight o'clock the smell from the roaster reached temptingly into every nook and cranny of the big store, even drowning out the odors of kerosene, drying boots and tobacco smoke.

In one front corner of the store was the post office, a section with pigeonholes, lock boxes, and a small wicket window. Posters bearing the ugly visages of wanted bank robbers, counterfeiters and railway post office bandits were tacked on the wall nearby, jostling for space with notices of strawberry festivals, auctions, stallions at stud and field dog trials.

Anyone dropping in for a last look for mail had to be uncommonly stouthearted to leave without buying a sack of peanuts.

The back room, unlike the main store, was strictly a man's world. The ladies took it for granted that it was out of bounds to them. Sometimes little girls with their pinafores all starched and their hair in pigtails would peek in longingly, but they never dared cross the threshold. Their brothers, however, strutted bravely past them—even if they did immediately subside and sit down quietly behind their fathers.

From that store, with its hand-turned coffee grinder, its drawers of spices, its jars and bins and shelves, came everything that went into Grandma's cakes and soups and other gustatory delights save what could be grown in her garden patch, Grandpa's fields or raised on the place. It was greengrocery, delicatessen, spice shop and supermarket all in one.

One of these homespun delicacies was Grandma's blackberry jam cake. It was light, yet moist. It was zesty without being too highly spiced. It was, in short, so satisfying to a man's tastebuds that someone should have written an ode about it.

The ingredients were a half cup of butter, a cup of brown sugar, three eggs, one and three-quarter cups of flour, one teaspoon of soda, a half teaspoon of ground cloves, one teaspoon each of cinnamon and nutmeg, one cup of blackberry jam, three tablespoons of sour milk, and a half cup of chopped raisins.

The old lady creamed the butter, added the brown sugar gradually and beat it with a spoon until it was fluffy. Then she added the beaten egg yolks, sifted the flour, soda and spices together, and added this mixture alternately with the jam and the sour milk. Next came the raisins, well floured. Last of all the beaten egg whites were folded in and the batter poured into two tins for a double layer cake. It was baked in a moderately hot oven.

Grandma mixed one and a half cups of confectioner's sugar,

three tablespoons of cream, and six tablespoons of butter for the frosting and filling.

She allowed the mixture to stand over hot water for fifteen minutes, added a teaspoon of vanilla extract and then spread it over the cake layers.

This blackberry jam cake was wonderful the first day and even more mouthwatering the second day, but it was never known to last long enough for anyone to learn what it would be like on the third day.

The old lady knew the grocer's stock almost as well as he did. She ordered a supply of horehound tablets in the late fall, to be ready for winter colds, and never was without enough mustard to make mustard plasters if Grandpa got rheumatiz in his back muscles from hauling and sawing wood.

Although she usually prepared her own pickles there were times when she sent for a few, and I had to walk back up the hill with special care so the brine wouldn't spill out from the little boat-like dish made of thinly split wood in which the storekeeper packed them before wrapping it in glazed butcher's paper.

Looking back at the days long gone by, I know now that the old lady must have hankered occasionally for something she hadn't cooked and fixed herself. Most good cooks feel the same way, becoming a little bored even with their own superior products.

I can remember one of Grandma's regular purchases at the store because the box was so handsome. It was dried apples. The cardboard box in which they came pictured fruit far redder and rounder than Grandpa's Winesaps.

Each fall she used to pare and slice apples and string the rings on clean twine. Then she dried them, sometimes in the sun and sometimes behind the stove, with cheesecloth wrapped around the strands to keep them clean. It was a slow process and no matter how many she dried it always seemed that by late March she was forced to buy the commercial fruit at the general store.

Whether she used her own or the bought apples, this was how she made dried apple pudding:

One cup of the dried fruit was rinsed and soaked overnight in just enough water to cover. In the morning the apples were cut into bits and mixed with the same water in which they had soaked. A cup of dark molasses, a teaspoon of cinnamon and a half teaspoon of ground cloves were added to the apples. Then Grandma mixed an egg, two chunks of butter the size of butter-nuts, and one and a fourth cups of flour. A teaspoon of baking soda was stirred in, the other ingredients added and stirred well and the whole pudding placed in a moderate oven to bake for forty-five minutes at 325°.

We ate it hot out of the oven, crowned with a sauce made of a half cup of butter creamed into a cup of sugar and flavored with cinnamon.

Grandma thought it especially valuable as a late winter dish and we had it most often when the ice was breaking up in the fulling-mill pond and the roads beginning to buckle with the early thaws. It was a spring tonic no one ever balked at taking.

Of course one reason why it tasted so good was the freshness of the ingredients. The eggs Grandma used had usually been plucked out of the nests, almost out from under the Rhode Island Reds before they stopped cackling. The milk had been given up the evening before, or that very morning, by Grandpa's sweet-natured, well-fed Jerseys. The old lady demanded fresh spices, and at least once a year went through the spice cabinet tossing out most of those remaining and replacing them with new purchases.

If the recipe called for grated nutmeg, she took a whole nutmeg and rubbed it up and down on her small nutmeg grater rather than use commercially prepared flavoring. She ground her peppercorns in a mill for ground pepper, and she used butter she had churned herself but a few days before.

All this care paid off. You could tell the difference from the first bite to the last.

Chapter 18

The Race for the Purse

WINTER came to Windham County well before Thanksgiving Day, no matter what the almanac or the calendar said. One day everything would be bleak and brown; the next morning the countryside would be blanketed with white, as snow came drifting down like feathers from a torn bed-tick. From November on, winds blew hard, drifts piled deep along the fences and stone walls, and the mercury grew increasingly sluggish about climbing out of the bottom of the glass.

Grandma and Grandpa didn't mind the snow at all. The old man raked leaves up to the foundations of the house and barn and packed the earliest drifts on top of them. This insulated the buildings against the sub-zero draughts and helped keep everything inside cozy and warm. So far as travel went, Grandpa had no worries. He preferred to move on runners instead of wheels, even though he owned the only automobile for miles around.

He had a trim sleigh with graceful lines, a swan's neck dash and real leather upholstery. He kept it polished and shiny, and as soon as harvesting was over he kept it in position just inside the doors of the carriage house, like a fire engine in the city. At the first hint of cold weather, when the frosts at night set the oak leaves to shivering, the old gentleman started watching the sky like a mariner, taking frequent readings of the thermometer and barometer on the side porch and behaving as if he had chiggers or the seven-year itch. The reason for his strange behavior was really very simple.

Each year the bank in the county seat gave a handsome purse to the first man who drove into town a distance of ten miles in a sleigh.

All over the county Yankee farmers with sporting blood seething behind granite-hard exteriors waited for the first snow, ready to hitch up. Sometimes they'd get the shafts up, the harness on and the doors open before enough snow fell to fill a talcum powder tin. There were many false starts, many propitious getaways that ended ignobly with the end of the snowfall or a sudden thaw. Many a farmer found the snow running out before he'd gone a few miles and had to bring the sleigh back home on a wagon to avoid damaging the iron-bound runners.

Grandpa won the purse four times. Grandma claimed it was because his rheumatism gave him a twelve-hour start on a change in the weather. Even if he was sound asleep he'd rouse up on those first winter nights, draw on his britches over his outing flannel nightshirt, don felt boots and a Mackinaw and be ready to give the bays the whip if snow started to fall.

Once he'd made the run into town—win or lose—he relaxed, and it was then that the youngsters started pestering him for a sleigh ride. He had a big boxwagon on bobs in which he hauled feed and firewood. It had plank seats, and on the evening of the sleigh ride he'd pack the bed of the wagon a foot thick with oat straw and hay.

A dozen or fourteen boys and girls, evenly paired, made a good crowd. In those days before snow suits and ski pants the girls wore three or four petticoats, homemade out of worn woolen blankets or quilted with satin and cotton batting. They wore gaiters, buttoned from ankle or shoe-top to way up there, heavy coats, knitted toques, mittens, and veils to protect their faces if the temperature dropped down around zero or the winds were sharp. The boys bundled up too, and pulled down the fur-lined flaps on their hunting caps.

Grandpa used the big Morgans to pull the sled. When they settled themselves and pushed against the big collars they could snap the big wagon free even if the runners were frozen fast.

The favorite route crossed the covered bridge over the She-tucket to Scotland Dam, on to Canterbury, and back through Franklin and along the ridge road to Kick Hill and home. Everyone started out sitting on the plank seats but after a while, the cold wind, whipping across the snowy fields, set the merrymakers to burrowing down into the hay, all wrapped up in blankets like cocoons.

It was open-air bundling, to tell the blunt truth, and anyone who says it wasn't never went on a sleigh ride. Grandpa knew what was going on but was too busy slapping his arms across his chest and keeping the team from wallowing in deep drifts to interfere, and I don't think he wanted to anyway.

Once we got home and pulled the straw out of our ears and necks and clothes Grandma was ready with mashed-potato doughnuts, hot from the iron kettle, and rolled in powdered sugar.

To make them Grandma beat two eggs until they were light and fluffy, added them to a cup of sugar and a half teaspoon of ground nutmeg and whipped it into a cupful of mashed potatoes. Then she sifted together four cups of flour, three teaspoons of baking powder and a teaspoon of salt. Next she stirred a half teaspoon of baking soda into a cup of buttermilk and mixed it and the dry ingredients into the mashed potato mixture. Finally she beat in three chunks of butter, each the size of a bantam's egg.

She chilled the dough, rolled it on a floured board, until it was a half inch thick. She seemed to know by the springiness of the dough just when to quit with the rolling pin and use the doughnut cutter.

Grandma had the big iron kettle on the front of the stove in time to have the deep fat pulsating with heat, but not yet sending off wisps of smoke. The doughnuts were dropped one by one into the fat and turned frequently with a long fork until they achieved a rich golden brown. Then they were removed and put in a strainer to drain.

There were always Fruit Hermits on hand, made at least four days earlier to allow for "ripening." This is how the old lady made them:

She let a half cup of butter stand in a mixing bowl until soft and pliable. Then she added a half cup of white sugar, a half cup of brown sugar, an egg, a fourth of a cup of sour milk, three-fourths of a cup of halved seeded raisins, and a half cup each of sliced dates and chopped butternuts, and a fourth of a cup of chopped citron.

Next she sifted together one and a half cups of flour, a half teaspoon of salt, one teaspoon of baking powder, a fourth teaspoon of soda, a half teaspoon of cinnamon, and a pinch of nutmeg and ground cloves. This she stirred into the other mixture, mixed it well, and dropped it by the teaspoonful on a greased baking sheet. She flattened them with a wet knife and baked them on the top rack of a moderate oven for ten or twelve minutes.

With fresh cider they were delicious. With hot cocoa they were wonderful. With hot tea they melted in your mouth. But any way at all, any time of the year, they left you thanking your stars for Grandma.

Chapter 19

The Ducks Fly South

INSIDE the front door of Grandma's house was a deer head mounted on the wall, with a rack underneath for Grandpa's twelve-gauge shotgun and his single-shot rifle.

About the time of year when the ground was so well frozen nothing but a January thaw would soften it, one or the other of the firearms would be missing from its place almost every morning. Then occasional thunder claps from the woodlot or the high pasture would explain why the old man was late for breakfast.

When he came stomping into the kitchen with a brace of

pheasant or a good catch of rabbits, his face looked like a russet apple in a bright light. Grandma was smart enough to praise him, being a darned good psychologist long before she ever heard the term used in Windham County. Even in those days free meat was not to be sneezed at.

The secret of Grandma's way of cooking pheasant lay in her use of juniper berries, which she sent me out to collect every fall, after they'd been dried in the sun and tempered by the early frosts.

She crushed the berries, added bacon fat and rubbed it on the breasts before laying the pheasant in an open roasting pan. After sprinkling them with pepper and salt—the former freshly ground in the little pepper mill that had once done duty on a clipper ship out of Stonington Harbor—she slid the pan into the oven of the big wood stove.

For as long as it took the meat to become succulent and tender, Grandma basted the pheasant breasts with a cup of cider and the juice formed from pan drippings.

Grandpa was a hard-working man and never one for wasting daylight hours, but it always seemed to me that he found plenty of excuses for being in the kitchen when the intoxicating smell of pheasant, cider and juniper juice came pouring out into the room each time the oven door was opened. At such times Grandpa kept the wood box filled to overflowing.

While magic was being performed inside the stove, Grandma braised the wings, thighs and other parts of the birds, putting them away to cool when they were done. Several days after the breasts had been eaten the old lady picked the braised meat off the bones, diced it and added it to several cups of gravy.

All this went into the top of a double boiler and was cooked slowly on the back of the stove while Grandma made fresh buttermilk biscuits. By the time the biscuits were lifted, brown and flaky, from the oven, the meat and gravy were piping hot. Splitting the biscuits, she laid them out on her biggest platter and poured the hot gravy over the lightly buttered halves.

This pheasant shortcake was Grandpa's favorite, and mine too, but for different reasons. Grandpa's store teeth were an aggravation and there was nothing in the shortcake to give him cause for worry or embarrassment. When the pheasant season was over, Grandma substituted chicken for the wild bird but it never tasted quite so good. There was something about the slightly gamy flavor of the pheasant and the exotic tang of the juniper berries that lifted it out of the ruck of ordinary foods, no matter how well prepared.

Rabbit pie was dirt cheap and as common as crabgrass in August when I grew up in Windham County. Grandma made it in this fashion:

She soaked the cleaned rabbits overnight in salted water. In the morning she cut them into serving pieces, tossed them into a kettle along with a handful of celery tops, a few sprigs of parsley, a couple of onions, diced, and a bay leaf. With water to cover, the meat simmered slowly until tender, when a dash of salt was added to the rabbit liquor.

Next, Grandma placed the meat in an earthenware baking crock and went to work on the remainder of the dish. She melted three tablespoons of butter, and added a like amount of flour, in a graniteware stewpan into which she poured the juice from the rabbit, straining it through a fine sieve. When it was smooth and somewhat thickened, she added cooked peas and carrots and poured the mixture over the pieces of rabbit.

Over the top went biscuit dough and into the oven went the baking dish. When the crust was well browned, the crock reappeared and was set down on the red and white checkered tablecloth in front of Grandpa. He did the serving.

When the November winds rattled the windows and brought the high-flying ducks down from Canada on their way to the distant canebrakes and tidal marshes of the South, Grandpa used to go to bed extra early. Grandma, on the other hand, stayed up extra late to keep the stove going good and hot and to pack a breakfast that would stay the old man's hunger while he waited in a duck blind over on Scotland Pond.

Grandma said she never minded this occasional chore. She claimed it gave her a good reason for staying up late. Sometimes I would notice her looking out of the window across the fields to where other houses stood silent under the cold moon.

It wasn't until I was nearly grown that I learned the reason behind Grandma's interest in things nocturnal.

"You can tell who's courting who," she explained years later. "Jest watch the tops of the chimneys. If sparks come shooting out late at night someone's sitting by the fireplace and tossing on wood. It's as clear as spring water. Married folks are in bed long gone."

To get back to Grandpa, snoring blissfully under warm blankets and the Steps-to-the-White-House quilt. He awoke by intuition, put on enough clothes in the frigid bedroom to be decent, and went out to the kitchen to finish dressing. By false dawn he was gone, and an hour later he was sitting in his blind, with long-handled flannel underwear, two sweaters, a Mackinaw coat, and gum boots to ward off the chilblains.

If he was lucky, he'd bring back a good bag of mallards or blacks or, rarely, a Canadian honker. He used to pluck, clean and singe the birds and hand them over with never a pin feather showing. Then it was up to Grandma.

She stuffed wild duck with apples, a little chopped celery and a handful of seedless raisins. Then she rubbed it all over with butter and plumped it into the oven to roast. Grandma thought wild duck should be roasted to bring out the true flavor. She basted it with a mixture of melted butter and hot water. Other cooks used orange juice or wine with good effect but neither of these methods had Grandma's approval for duck.

With this delicacy the old lady always served wild rice, steamed until fluffy, and seasoned with butter and cayenne pepper. Any other accompaniment would have been as unthinkable as stirring cake batter in more than one direction. Nothing good would have come from it.

Chapter 20

Bless This Meal—and Grandma

ONCE a year Grandma cleared everything off the top shelf in the buttery and baked enough mince pies to run from one end to the other. Then we knew that Thanksgiving was just over the horizon.

On the day we saw her peeling a great dish full of white onions, a piece of hard bread held in her teeth, but with the tears streaming down her face nonetheless, we were sure the holiday was just one day off. Grandma always peeled onions the day before Thanksgiving so her eyes wouldn't look as if she'd been crying when the relations came to dinner.

The sweet old lady swore that the crust of bread was supposed to prevent the tears, but to a small boy it looked as if Grandma's lachrymal plumbing had been connected to the kitchen pump by mistake.

Tears notwithstanding, by then she had brought out the pink lusterware from the top shelf of the china closet and washed a year's dust from it, polished the good silver, and gathered together the russet apples, the Grimes Goldens, the Winesaps, the butternuts and chestnuts, the Bartlett pears and a few red ears of Indian field corn to make a centerpiece.

A small boy arises early on Thanksgiving in New England, but it always seemed that Grandma had been up for hours. She bustled about the big kitchen at a pace that belied her age.

In Windham County cooks had to get up early because by tradition the festive board groaned under this assortment of good things to eat: dried corn soup, turkey, stuffing, celery, (which stood upright in a tumbler like a vase of flowers), giblet gravy, mashed potatoes, mashed yellow turnips, boiled onions, pan rolls, cranberry sauce, sweet green tomato preserves, mince and squash pies.

Grandpa scoffed at pumpkin pie. "Punkin," he snorted, "should be fed to the cattle."

Grandma needed a thirty-pound tom turkey to cope with the appetites her relatives brought with them to our home. She was the only woman I ever knew who baked the bird—stuffed to overflowing with tasty dressing—with a cloth over it to prevent premature browning.

She called the cloth the turkey's diaper and dipped it in hot water and melted butter, wrung it out, and spread it over the fowl, tucking it in around the sides. Every few minutes she basted the bird, keeping the diaper moist until the last twenty minutes. Then the cloth was removed so the turkey would turn a rich, tawny color no artist this side of Heaven could duplicate.

We knew nothing about hors d'oeuvres in Windham County. The sole item allowed to precede the servings of the turkey itself was dried corn soup, and only a medium-sized cup at that. No one wanted to reach the main course carrying any more baggage than neccessary.

Grandma dried the corn herself in the late summer. The night before Thanksgiving she soaked it all night with just a pinch of salt added to the water.

In the morning she started it simmering and when the kernels were tender she added diced salt pork that had been browned in a skillet, finely chopped onions, and a little pepper. Then a quart of milk for every two cups of corn was stirred in just before time to serve it.

Grandma had her own little tricks, like any other Yankee cook. She always cooked a medium white potato with each two-pound turnip which she said made the mashed turnips immeasurably lighter. When she whipped them, the way she used butter to make them fluffy was a caution to see. She used dark Jamaica rum to give tang to her mincemeat, and she waited until the last possible minute to bake her squash pies. Her cranberry sauce, made the day before the holiday, was never strained and bore no resemblance to today's cylindrical gelatin.

By noontime the aunts and uncles, the brothers and sisters, the cousins and second cousins began arriving. If there was snow on the road, and there usually was, they came in sleighs and the sound of the bells sent a small boy's blood pressure up beyond all safe limits.

Grandpa helped unharness the horses, strap blankets on them and turn them into the stables. It was my job to shake the snow off the lap robes and hang them on pegs in the woodshed where the laundry stove was kept going to dry them out.

While the men did their best to keep from under foot, the women folk put on their prettiest aprons and gave Grandma some last minute assistance. To a small boy it seemed as if they really wanted an excuse to get close to the big kitchen stove, which sent out heat in great waves every time the oven door was opened to baste the turkey, or the firebox opened to toss in another stick of white birch.

No one had to be called to dinner. It was as if a mystic signal went out at the precise instant Grandma transferred the turkey from the oven to the huge platter.

Grandpa stood up to ask the Lord's blessing and he stayed on his feet to carve—an accomplishment of which he was mighty proud. Everyone talked at once and Grandma looked across the table, so loaded with food the beautiful linen cloth with the eagle and shield woven into the fabric was hidden from sight, and nodded in a self-satisfied way.

No one paid any attention when a small boy, almost submerged in a sea of skirts and Sunday-go-to-meeting suits, loosened his belt a couple of notches, just in case.

PAGES FROM GRANDMA'S
RECIPE BOOK

Grandma always cooked to feed four to six hungry mouths. Unless otherwise stated, most of the following recipes are designed to serve five or six.

Chapter 21

Soups, Chowders, and Stews

CORN CHOWDER

2 tablespoons salt pork, diced
1 large onion, diced
4 cups potatoes, diced

1 pint boiling water
2 cups canned or fresh corn
1 pint rich milk

salt and pepper

Cut salt pork into small pieces. Chop onion. Boil diced potatoes
in boiling water for 15 minutes. Fry salt pork and onion together for 2 minutes. Add these ingredients and corn to
potatoes and cook until potatoes are done. Add milk and

season to taste with salt and pepper. Bring mixture to boiling point. Serve very hot.

SPLIT PEA SOUP

1 pound split peas, yellow or green

3 quarts cold water

1 pound lightly salted pork shoulder

1 small ham bone

1 medium-sized onion

2 tablespoons minced parsley

3 peppercorns

Sort peas carefully for foreign material and wash in cold water. Soak peas in cold water overnight. Put on to cook in same water adding salted pork cut into small chunks. Add ham bone (or a piece of a large one), onion, parsley and peppercorns. Let simmer for 3 hours or more, adding water as needed to keep amount up to 3 quarts. When done, the soup will be medium thick with little pieces of savory meat in it. Remove ham bone and serve very hot.

This soup is even better when reheated, and it may be prepared a day or two in advance if kept under refrigeration.

CABBAGE SOUP or COUNTRY SOUP

1 firm head of young cabbage

1 big onion

3 tablespoons melted butter

1 tablespoon flour

1 cup sour cream

3 cups soup stock

salt and pepper

Cut cabbage into small pieces with sharp knife. Boil for exactly 5 minutes in furiously boiling water sufficient to cover. Chop onion and simmer it gently in melted butter until yellow as gold. Shake in flour and blend well, taking pot off stove for this process. Return to stove and add sour cream, stirring constantly. Then add gradually soup stock (canned consommé or bouillon may be substituted but is not as good) and continue stirring until smooth. Add boiled cabbage, which has been well drained, and season to taste. Heat thoroughly without boiling. Serve very hot.

JUGGED SOUP

Carcasses of cold fowl, or bones
  of roast meat or steak
3 quarts water
6 medium-large potatoes, sliced
  very thin
1 onion, sliced
2 cups canned tomatoes

1 small turnip, sliced thin
1 cup peas, canned or frozen
1 carrot, grated
¼ cup raw rice
1 tablespoon salt
1 tablespoon sugar
½ teaspoon pepper

1 pinch allspice

Boil carcasses of cold fowl, or bones from meat with trimmings, in water until it is reduced to 2 quarts. Strain, cool, and lift off fat. Lay potatoes in earthenware jar (1 gallon size), with lid. Place on these onion, 1 cup tomatoes, turnip, peas, carrot, another cup of tomatoes and rice. On each layer as it is added sprinkle seasoning made by mixing salt, sugar, pepper and allspice. Then pour broth over all, put on lid and cover edges with a flour paste to keep in the steam. Set jar in pan of hot water and put it in oven to cook for from 4 to 6 hours at 275°. When done, pour into tureen and serve with crisped crackers.

QUAHOG CHOWDER

1 pint hard quahog clams	1 quart boiling water
¼ pound salt pork, diced	freshly ground black pepper
2 onions, sliced	2 cups milk, half cream
4 medium-sized potatoes	⅛ pound butter

Remove clams from shells. Save liquor. Put quahogs through coarse food grinder. Try out pork until brown and crisp around edges and tender. Brown onions in same skillet. Cut up potatoes into small pieces or dice them and boil until tender. Add quahogs, pork and onions to potatoes. Then add liquor, as much as needed to taste. Too little is bad; too much may leave chowder too salty. Each cook must learn the family's preference. Sprinkle on fresh pepper and cook all until clams are tender.

This chowder is good eaten at once, with the rich milk added and butter stirred in just before serving. But any Yankee knows it is better if allowed to stand in glass jars overnight in the refrigerator, then warmed up and the milk and butter added in time to become hot with the rest. The overnight seasoning is well worth the extra effort.

CONNECTICUT FISH CHOWDER

4 pounds haddock or cod	3 large onions, diced
6 cups cold water	2 stalks celery, chopped fine
1 bay leaf	2 tablespoons flour
3 sprigs parsley, diced	3 medium-sized potatoes, diced
½ pound salt pork, chopped fine	3 cups milk
salt and pepper	

Wash, clean, bone and cut up fish. Place head and bones in deep kettle. Cover with cold water, add bay leaf and parsley.

Cover. Simmer slowly 20 minutes. Then strain carefully. While this is cooking, try out salt pork in heavy skillet. Pick out pork pieces when brown, and drain. To drippings in skillet add onion and celery and cook until onion is gold colored and clear. Then blend in flour thoroughly. Add fish broth and potatoes. Cook slowly 15 minutes. Then add diced, boned fish and simmer until fish is tender (about 10 minutes). Add milk and drained pieces of pork. Heat thoroughly but do not boil. Season to taste with salt and pepper.

If this chowder is reheated, and it is equally good the second day, use double boiler to make it very hot but do not boil or scorch it.

LOBSTER STEW, NIANTIC STYLE

6 lobsters, averaging 1 pound each	2 quarts milk
	1 pint light cream
2 cups boiling water	salt and pepper
¼ pound fresh butter	Pilot crackers

Lay cleaned lobsters, shell side down, in boiling water in large kettle. Cover tightly and steam at high heat 15 minutes. While lobsters are still hot, pick meat from shell, discarding lungs and intestinal veins. Put lobster meat in glass dish, cover and refrigerate overnight or an equal period of time. When ready to make chowder, melt butter in large cooking pot; add lobster meat; cook until it bubbles merrily. Then lower heat and slowly add 1 quart milk, stirring constantly. Bring almost to a boil. Then add second quart of milk very slowly, stirring all the while. Let it come to a boil. Then add cream; simmer uncovered (do not boil) for about 3 minutes. Remove from heat. Serve with Pilot crackers.

To obtain an even better flavor cool and refrigerate the lobster stew for 12 hours or more and then reheat and serve.

HALE PLACE SOUP

1 cup dried split peas	1 tablespoon rice
or	1 medium-sized carrot, diced
1 cup cranberry beans	2 medium-sized onions,
8 cups boiling water	chopped
1 pound stewing lamb, cut in	1 tablespoon dried parsley
small chunks	1 pinch salt

Pick over peas or beans carefully, wash, and put to soak overnight. In the morning drain, put into boiling water, add other ingredients and pour into covered bean pot. Place pot in slow oven (about 300°) and cook evenly for 4 hours. Many cooks prefer to use water in which peas were soaked overnight so as not to lose minerals and flavor. If this is done, reduce amount of boiling water by the quantity of water left from soaking.

DRIED CORN SOUP

2 cups dried corn	2 medium-sized onions,
1 pinch salt	chopped fine
¼ pound lean salt pork	fresh ground pepper
1 quart milk	

Soak corn in enough salted water to cover overnight. In the morning simmer corn in same water until kernels are tender, adding a little water if needed. Try out salt pork which has been diced in skillet until golden brown in color. Add chopped onions and dash of pepper. Stir this into corn and then add milk, stirring until hot.

BEAN CHOWDER

1 cup dried beans
¾ cup lean salt pork, chopped fine
1 medium-sized onion, chopped fine
1 cup potatoes, chopped
1 cup chopped celery and celery leaves

2½ cups tomatoes
3 sprigs parsley, chopped
1 cup water
2 tablespoons flour
2 cups hot milk
salt and pepper

Soak beans overnight in enough water to cover. Cook in same water until tender. Drain and place on back of stove. Cook together in heavy kettle salt pork and onion until lightly browned. Add potatoes, celery, tomatoes, parsley and beans. Add cup of water. Cover kettle and simmer until vegetables are tender. Thicken with flour mixed to a paste with a little cold water. Add hot milk and season to taste.

POTATO SOUP

3 cups raw potatoes, diced
¾ cup celery, cut fine
½ cup onions, cut fine
5 cups rich milk

5 tablespoons butter
¼ teaspoon black pepper
paprika and parsley to garnish

1 teaspoon salt

Cook potatoes, celery and onions in *just* enough boiling water to cover. When tender, most of water will be absorbed by vegetables. Over very low heat bring milk *almost* to a boil. Add cooked vegetables to milk with whatever cooking water is left. Put in butter, salt and pepper. Again bring to a boil, being careful not to scorch milk. Shake in a little paprika and finely chopped parsley if desired. Serve very hot.

Chapter 22

Fish

KEDGEREE

3 cups hot rice	½ cup rich milk
3 tablespoons butter	5 hard-boiled eggs, chopped
3 cups cooked flaked fish, scallops	2 sprigs fresh parsley,
or lobster chunks	chopped

salt and pepper

Season rice with a little salt and pepper. Then mix butter into it and add flaked fish or shellfish, milk, chopped eggs, parsley and a little Hungarian paprika if this color is desired. Heat

118

thoroughly over hot water. Any good fish can be used but cod and haddock are most common. A more piquant taste can be achieved by using flaked fish and shellfish together. Any combination works well.

CODFISH BALLS

1½ cups shredded salt codfish
3 cups raw potatoes, diced
1 egg, beaten

2 tablespoons butter
¼ teaspoon pepper
fat for frying

Soak salt codfish overnight in plenty of water. Drain in the morning and soak again for 1 hour. Drain again. Place flaked codfish and diced potatoes in pot and cook until potatoes are tender. Drain off water. Mash egg and butter together, add pepper and then add to potatoes and fish. Beat well together. Drop mixture from cooking spoon into shallow fat which is hot enough to brown a small piece of white bread in less than 1 minute. Fry until a rich golden brown. Drain on rack or absorbent paper.

CREAMED FINNAN HADDIE

1 short thick finnan haddie
3 tablespoons butter
3 tablespoons flour
1 pint milk

¼ teaspoon salt
¼ teaspoon pepper
1 tablespoon butter
1 sprig parsley, finely chopped
paprika, to garnish

Soak finnan haddie in warm water for 20 minutes. Drain. Cover with cold water and simmer slowly for 30 minutes. Drain. Remove skin and bones. Flake flesh of fish into medium-large chunks. Make sauce by blending together in top of double boiler 3 tablespoons butter and flour. Slowly add milk, stirring constantly until thickened. Cook over hot water for 5 minutes. Add seasonings, then the fish. Cook about 10 minutes longer. Just before serving add 1 tablespoon butter, and parsley. Paprika, sprinkled lightly over fish, helps alter the dull coloring of the dish.

SCALLOPED OYSTERS

1 quart raw oysters	½ teaspoon black pepper
¼ cup butter	⅛ teaspoon red pepper
2 cups toasted bread crumbs	1 teaspoon Worcestershire
¼ teaspoon salt	sauce
	4 tablespoons cream

Strain liquor from oysters and save it. Pick over oysters very carefully, removing bits of shell. Melt butter. Add toasted crumbs and mix gently but thoroughly. Cover bottom of baking dish with about a third of buttered crumbs. Next gently lay half of oysters on bed of crumbs. Combine oyster liquor with salt, peppers, cream and Worcestershire sauce. Pour half of sauce over oysters. Then cover this with toasted crumbs, then remainder of oysters. Use remaining crumbs for a top layer and pour remaining liquid sauce over all. Bake uncovered at 425° for 30 minutes.

CAPE COD TURKEY

1 pound salt codfish	2 cups milk
4 tablespoons butter	2 eggs, well beaten
4 tablespoons flour	¼ teaspoon black pepper

Soak salt codfish in cold water for several hours, or, better yet, overnight. Drain. Pour fresh cold water over fish. Bring to boiling point. Drain and flake fish. Melt butter in top of double boiler over boiling water. Blend in flour. Then slowly add milk, stirring constantly until thickened. Add a little of this white sauce to eggs. Then blend this mixture slowly into white sauce in double boiler, stirring constantly. Add codfish flakes and pepper. Cook for 3 minutes.

This is one of the commonest dishes in all New England. It was used to pour over toast, boiled potatoes and rice, or was eaten alone, in the early colonial days. With the growth of quick-process foods, it has not always been so popular in late years, but in many Yankee homes it still is one of the prime favorites.

BAKED COD STEAKS

2 pounds cod steak	½ cup bread crumbs
1 lemon	2½ tablespoons butter

SAUCE

2 tablespoons butter	¼ teaspoon nutmeg
2 tablespoons flour	½ teaspoon salt
½ tablespoon dry mustard	¼ teaspoon black pepper
1 cup hot milk	

Make sauce first. Melt butter. Mix flour with other dry ingredients. Blend mixture into butter. Slowly add hot milk while stirring, and cook over low heat until thickened, still stirring all the time. Place fish in buttered baking dish. Squeeze juice from lemon over it. Then cover with sauce. On top of this put bread crumbs. Dot thoroughly with butter. Bake uncovered at 350° for about 35 minutes. A little paprika should be dusted over dish before serving.

SHAD ROE WITH BACON

1 pair shad roe

1 small onion, sliced

1 teaspoon cider vinegar

6 whole peppercorns

3 whole Jamaica allspice

1 bay leaf

1 teaspoon salt

4 slices bacon

Place shad roe in heavy skillet. Add seasonings and onion. Cover with boiling water. Simmer, covered, very gently for 5 minutes. Remove pan from fire and cool for 10 minutes. In another heavy skillet cook bacon. When crisp and brown remove from fat and drain. Lift roe from its skillet and drain. Cook roe in hot bacon fat until nicely browned all over. Season to taste and serve with the bacon.

SCALLOP SALAD

4 cups cooked scallops

½ cup celery, in small pieces

2 hard-boiled eggs, chopped

2 tablespoons parsley, chopped
     fine

2 teaspoons vinegar

½ teaspoon salt

½ teaspoon black pepper

¼ teaspoon celery salt

Mix scallops well with celery, egg, parsley, vinegar and seasonings. Mix lightly with enough Boiled Mustard Dressing (see below) to moisten well. Serve on crisp lettuce leaves.

GRANDMA'S BOILED MUSTARD DRESSING

1 cup rich milk

2 egg yolks, beaten

3 teaspoons dry mustard

4 teaspoons sugar

2 teaspoons flour

1 teaspoon salt

¼ teaspoon black pepper

1 cup vinegar, heated

2 tablespoons butter

2 egg whites, stiffly beaten

Bring milk to boiling point. Add mixed dry ingredients to beaten egg yolks. Blend gently, stirring constantly, with milk. Pour hot vinegar slowly into this, stirring all the time. Cook this mixture until well thickened. Remove from fire. Add butter and beat well. Then fold in the stiffly beaten egg whites.

This is an old New England recipe, popular in many families for generations. It is a bit touchy to make but is well worth the attention to details because the flavor is so tantalizing. It is good for many uses, especially for summer dishes. It is used hot on hot dishes, and cold on cold foods.

FISH HASH

2 cups cooked fish, flaked	¼ teaspoon black pepper
2 cups cooked potatoes, chopped	salt to taste
2 tablespoons onions, minced	1 egg, beaten
fat for frying	

Mix ingredients together in the order given. Heat enough fat for frying in heavy skillet. Put in hash and cook until golden brown. Serve hot.

BAKED CONNECTICUT RIVER SHAD

1 shad, cleaned and split	4 tablespoons butter
1½ teaspoons salt	1 tablespoon parsley, chopped
1 teaspoon black pepper	fine
lemon slices	

Wash shad. Sprinkle with salt and pepper and put it in well-buttered baking dish. Dot all over with butter. Bake at 400° for 30 minutes, or until fish is done. Remove to hot platter. Sprinkle shad with parsley and serve with slices of lemon.

MRS. CLEVERLY'S CLAM FRITTERS

2 cups clams, drained	2 teaspoons baking powder
2 eggs, well beaten	¼ teaspoon salt
½ cup milk	¼ teaspoon black pepper
1½ cups flour	fat for frying

Chop clams fine. Blend eggs and milk together. Sift dry ingredients together and add milk mixture. Beat well. Add clams. Heat fat (about 1 inch deep) in heavy skillet. Drop clam mixture from spoon into hot fat. Brown on each side. Drain. Serve hot.

FISH AND ASPARAGUS CASSEROLE

1½ pounds fresh fish	2 teaspoons onions, chopped fine
hot water to cover	2 teaspoons celery, chopped fine
1 teaspoon salt	1 teaspoon parsley, chopped fine
1 bay leaf	¼ teaspoon salt
1 sprig thyme	¼ teaspoon pepper
3 tablespoons butter	1 cup green asparagus, cooked
3 tablespoons flour	½ cup bread crumbs
1½ cups hot milk	2½ tablespoons butter

Almost any fresh fish will do for this dish, but codfish, haddock or halibut are especially good. Cook fish in hot water with 1 teaspoon salt, bay leaf and thyme for 12 minutes. Drain and remove skin and bones from fish. Place fish in buttered baking dish. Make sauce by melting 3 tablespoons butter in saucepan, blending in flour and then adding hot milk, onion, celery, parsley, ¼ teaspoon salt and pepper. Stir until smooth and thick. Pour sauce over fish. Put asparagus on top of sauce and cover with bread crumbs. Dot generously with butter and bake at 400° for about 20 minutes, or until browned to taste. A little Hungarian paprika may be added for extra zest.

Chapter 23

Main Dishes

YANKEE POT ROAST

1 piece suet the size of a large
  coffee cup
4 or 5 pounds bottom round beef
4 medium-sized onions, chopped
  fine
2 medium-sized white turnips,
  diced
4 carrots, diced
2 cups celery, chopped
1 peeled fresh tomato or

1 solid tomato from can
3 sprigs parsley
1 scant tablespoon salt
½ teaspoon black pepper
½ teaspoon Hungarian
  paprika
1 cup cold water
6 medium-sized potatoes,
  cut up
  flour to thicken gravy

salt and pepper to taste

125

Melt suet in large, heavy pot. Then thoroughly brown piece of beef on all sides, keeping pot hot during process. Remove beef to platter. Put onions, turnips, carrots and celery in pot and stir until browned. Add tomato which has been cut fine and parsley. Replace meat, covering it with vegetables and sprinkling salt, pepper and paprika over it. Add 1 cup water and cover tightly. Cook very slowly either on top of stove or in slow oven (300°). Turn beef over once while cooking for 4 or 5 hours and until meat is tender. An hour before serving lay chunks of potatoes on top of meat to steam. When all is tender remove meat to hot platter and surround with potatoes and vegetable mixture. Add enough water to liquor in pot to make desired amount of gravy and thicken with flour.

VEAL STEW WITH DUMPLINGS

2½ pounds rump or shoulder veal	½ bay leaf
1½ quarts cold water	1 teaspoon salt
½ cup onion, chopped	¼ cup tomatoes, strained
½ cup celery, chopped	½ teaspoon sugar
	salt and pepper

Cut veal into 2-inch pieces. Cover with water. Add onion, celery, bay leaf and 1 teaspoon salt. Cover and simmer until meat is tender. Remove bay leaf. Add tomatoes and sugar; and season to taste with salt and pepper. Reheat and drop dumpling mixture by spoonfuls on top of meat. Cover and cook 15 minutes without removing lid. Lift out dumplings onto hot platter. Pour stew over them.

DUMPLINGS

2 cups flour
1 teaspoon salt
¾ teaspoon soda

3 tablespoons shortening (butter,
   lard or vegetable fat)
¾ cup sour milk

Sift dry materials together. Rub in the shortening. Add milk to make a soft dough. Place on top of stew and cover closely. Steam 15 minutes without removing lid and serve immediately.

SATURDAY NOON POT PIE

1 stewing chicken, 3 or 4 pounds
3 peppercorns
1 large stalk celery, scraped
1 large whole onion
1 large carrot, scraped
2 sprigs parsley

1 level tablespoon salt
2 cups bread dough
2 tablespoons butter
6 medium-sized potatoes
1 cup cold milk
   flour to thicken gravy

Clean chicken and cut into pieces for serving. Drop them into just enough boiling water to cover, to which peppercorns have been added. Next add celery, onion, carrot, parsley, salt. After water comes to a boil skim off carefully any froth that appears on top. Then lower heat and simmer, closely covered, taking care it does not boil dry. Add extra *boiling* water if needed.

While chicken is cooking, cut off about 2 cups of light bread dough, work butter into it and shape dough into small dumplings. Cover them and set in warm place to rise. Wash and pare potatoes, cutting to half the size of an egg. Parboil potatoes for 10 minutes in boiling salted water.

When chicken is almost done, remove celery, onion, carrot and peppercorns from kettle. Taste liquor and add seasoning if needed. Add potatoes to chicken; and when liquor begins to boil again, add milk. Then lay on the risen dumplings. Cover closely and steam for 20 minutes without removing lid. Take out dumplings and chicken; place on hot platter. Make gravy in usual manner, adding more milk if needed.

This chicken pot pie was called Saturday Noon Pot Pie because Grandma baked on Saturday and had the bread dough handy. It could cook while she baked and needed little attention.

SHIPWRECK

1 pound raw chopped beef
1 large onion, sliced thin
3 medium-sized potatoes, sliced thin
¼ cup uncooked rice

2 cups cooked red kidney beans
½ cup celery, sliced thin
1 can tomatoes rubbed through sieve
Hungarian paprika

salt and pepper

Slice onion into large buttered baking dish. Then place layer of paper-thin potato slices on top. Next place layers of chopped beef, uncooked rice, kidney beans and sliced celery in the dish. Blend tomatoes which have been strained with an equal amount of water and pour on top of ingredients. Salt and pepper it and sprinkle small amount of Hungarian paprika over all. Cover dish and place in oven. Cook for 2 hours at moderate heat (325°). If necessary add a little water during cooking, but do not make dish too moist.

BEEF STEW

½ cup suet, cut fine
2½ pounds lean beef (chuck or Boston round) cut into serving pieces
2 teaspoons salt
½ teaspoon pepper
1 sprig parsley

6 carrots, cut lengthwise
1 medium-sized turnip, diced
3 stalks celery, cut in bites
8 small whole onions
6 medium-sized potatoes, quartered
1 teaspoon Hungarian paprika

Melt suet in heavy kettle. Add beef and brown thoroughly. Add salt, pepper and parsley, and pour on boiling water to cover. Then cover kettle and cook slowly for about 2 hours or until meat is almost tender. Then add carrots and turnip and cook for about 15 minutes. Add celery, onions, and potatoes and cook until vegetables are done. Add water if needed during cooking. Add paprika just before taking up from stove. This is good with hot biscuits or homemade bread.

RED FLANNEL HASH

6 medium-sized beets, cooked
4 medium-sized potatoes, cooked
1 cup chopped corned beef,
　cooked
　salt and pepper

½ cup onion, very finely
　chopped
2 tablespoons butter
1 tablespoon cream
1 tablespoon butter

Peel and chop beets and potatoes. Mix together beets, potatoes, corned beef and onion. Stir in seasoning to taste. Heat 2 tablespoons butter in frying pan. Spread mixture over bottom of pan. Brown very slowly. When hash is nearly ready to serve add cream and 1 tablespoon butter. Finish browning quickly and when crust forms, turn out and serve.

PORK CHOPS IN CREAM GRAVY

4 medium thick lean pork chops
　salt, pepper and sugar

2 tablespoons flour
1½ cups fresh milk

Cut some fat from chops and melt it slowly in heavy frying pan. Wipe chops with damp cloth. Sprinkle them with salt and pepper and a tiny bit of sugar. Fry slowly in fat until browned on both sides. Cover very tightly and cook slowly, turning occasionally, for about 35 to 40 minutes, or until tender. Remove from pan to hot platter. Add flour to pan drippings and mix to a smooth paste. Then add milk and stir rapidly over moderate heat until smooth and thickened. Pour over chops and serve.

ROUND STEAK SMOTHERED IN ONIONS

3 pounds round steak	salt and pepper
1 tablespoon butter or bacon	2 tablespoons cider vinegar
drippings	3 sprigs parsley, chopped
6 onions, finely chopped	2 sprigs thyme
1 tablespoon flour	2 sprigs bay leaf
1 pint boiling water	

Beat round steak well with the edge of a small dish, rolling pin or steak-hammer. Melt butter in deep frying pan; then add onions. Dredge steak with flour and season with salt and pepper. Place in pan, surround with onions and cover closely. Simmer for a few minutes, then turn to other side. After 3 minutes add vinegar, parsley, thyme and bay leaf.

When steak is nicely browned, add boiling water which should cover meat. Then lower heat and allow to simmer gently for 2 hours. At serving time remove steak to hot platter and cover it with onions and gravy.

WAR OFFICE PIE

The name and history of this dish go back to the Revolutionary War. In the little village of Lebanon, Conn., there still stands a small building in which George Washington conferred with his generals, the Frenchman Rochambeau and Governor Jonathan Trumbull about the campaigns planned to end the war. The dish, based on mutton and tomatoes, was one of General Washington's favorites, and is well known in Connecticut and the South as well. No precise quantities are given, or needed, because it is made from leftovers.

bread crumbs	salt and pepper
cold roast mutton cut in chunks	butter
tomatoes	sugar

Cover bottom of baking dish with bread crumbs. Place on this a layer of mutton cut about the size of a bantam's egg. Over meat lay thick slices of red tomatoes. Then place second layer of bread crumbs, and more meat, and more tomatoes. Sprinkle each layer with salt and pepper and dot with butter. Make the top layer tomatoes, sprinkled over lightly with sugar and bread crumbs. Bake for 30 minutes in hot oven (400°). Firm canned tomatoes may be substituted for fresh ones.

RICE PIE

3 cups warm boiled rice	2 to 3 cups leftover meat,
4 tablespoons butter	diced, with gravy
1 egg, well beaten	2 hard-boiled eggs, sliced
1 pinch nutmeg	salt and pepper

While rice is still warm mix into it butter, egg, and nutmeg. Line casserole with part of rice and turn into it diced meat and gravy. If meat and gravy are already well seasoned, not much salt and pepper need be used. Add sliced eggs and cover with remaining rice. Bake in moderate oven (375°) for about 25 minutes.

SUMMER MEAT PIE

3½ to 4 cups cooked beef, diced
¼ cup finely chopped celery
2 tablespoons finely chopped onions
2 cups leftover gravy

salt and pepper
6 ripe fresh peaches
¼ cup strained tomato pulp seasoned with salt, pepper, 1 teaspoon sugar and 1 teaspoon vinegar

Place cut up beef, celery, onion and gravy in shallow baking dish. Sprinkle with salt and pepper. Cover and bake at 350° for about 20 minutes. Peel and halve peaches and remove stones. Fill centers with tomato pulp mixture. Place hollowed side down on top of meat. Cover and bake 20 minutes longer, or until peaches are done.

FIREMAN'S SUPPER

6 pork chops
4 medium-sized potatoes, sliced thin

4 medium-sized onions, sliced thin
salt and pepper

hot milk or hot water

Trim some fat from chops and melt in heavy frying pan. Brown chops slowly on both sides in this fat. Then cover well with raw sliced potatoes and onions. Season well. Fill pan with hot milk or hot water. Cover tightly and simmer slowly in oven or top of stove until potatoes are soft. This usually takes about 30 minutes.

RHODE ISLAND JOHNNYCAKE
AND DRIED BEEF GRAVY

2 cups white corn meal
1 teaspoon salt

3 cups boiling water
shortening for frying

Mix corn meal and salt in deep earthenware bowl. Slowly pour boiling water into it, stirring constantly so as to scald all of meal. As corn meal differs according to the way it's ground, it may take a little less, or a little more, than 3 cups of water. When mixture is well stirred, allow to set for 10 to 15 minutes, with bowl covered. Then meal should be so stiff it has to be pushed off spoon onto hot greased griddle. With pancake turner pat meal into flat cakes, about ⅜ of an inch thick. When one side is a rich brown, beginning to turn darker, turn and cook other side. The two sides should have a thick, nutty crust, and the inside should be cooked through. While cakes are frying, or before, prepare:

DRIED BEEF GRAVY

⅛ pound butter 2½ tablespoons flour
¼ pound dried beef 3 cups milk

Use deep frying pan or skillet. An iron or heavy aluminum one is better than a thin one. Melt butter and then break up dried beef into small pieces, the size of postage stamps. Brown beef slightly in butter, adding flour and working flour, beef and butter together. Add milk *very* slowly, stirring all the while until it forms a thick gravy. Keep hot on back of stove until johnnycakes are ready. Then pour some gravy over each cake as it is served.

This is one of the oldest and best loved of old New England recipes for corn meal. It makes up into a hearty meal with the gravy. Most old Yankees dashed a drop of cider vinegar on the gravy as they ate each cake. It is best to serve cakes as they are fried rather than to stack them up, although this means the cook waits until the end.

BAKED BEANS

Cranberry beans were preferred by Grandma, but red kidney beans were a good second choice. White pea beans were considered good only for unfortunate folk who didn't care what they ate, but some of Grandma's neighbors ate them with no bad results. Bacon can be substituted for the salt pork in this recipe. If it is used, cut the strips into fourths and place them with the seasonings all through the beans, instead of on top.

1 pound cranberry beans	1 tablespoon butter
cold water to cover	1 teaspoon prepared mustard
½ cup dark brown sugar	1 large onion, sliced thin
½ teaspoon salt	¼ pound lean salt pork
½ teaspoon black pepper	1 teaspoon white sugar

Pick over the beans carefully; wash, drain and soak overnight in sufficient cold water to cover. In the morning cook slowly in same water until the skins crinkle and break. Drain beans, reserving liquor. Put a layer of beans into earthenware bean pot. Sprinkle with some of the brown sugar, salt, pepper, butter, mustard and sliced onion. Repeat process until pot is almost full, making sure the top layer is made up of beans. Pour boiling water over salt pork. Scrape the rind and score it. Press pork into beans, leaving a small corner above the surface. Then pour bean liquor over all. There should be enough liquor so that it will come on top and show above the beans. If there is not enough, add what hot water is needed to gain same result. Sprinkle with white sugar, cover, and bake in a slow oven (275°) for 6 hours or until beans are done. It may take even longer. During the process it may be necessary to add a little hot water now and again. If the beans are preferred with a crusty layer on top, uncover the pot for the last half-hour of

baking. Serve with Aunt Annie's Chili Sauce (see page 229).
This is good with Steamed Brown Bread (see page 158).

SHEPHERD'S PIE

2 cups mashed potatoes, hot
2 cups cooked chopped lamb
2 cups gravy
¼ teaspoon pepper

1 teaspoon salt
2 tablespoons butter
¼ teaspoon paprika
1 teaspoon onion juice

Line bottom of buttered baking dish with potato. Add a generous layer of chopped lamb and gravy. Add another layer of potato and another of lamb until all is used. Season each layer with salt and pepper. Be sure to make top layer mashed potatoes. Dot with butter and sprinkle with paprika (Hungarian paprika is best). Some cooks don't like onion juice, but it adds zest. If used, mix with gravy before arranging layers. Bake in hot oven (400°) until crust is golden brown.

AUNT RACHAEL'S STEW

6 lean pork chops
6 tablespoons raw rice
6 tablespoons chopped onion
6 slices fresh red tomatoes

6 slices green pepper
salt and pepper
Hungarian paprika
2 tablespoons flour

3 cups boiling water

Brown pork chops on both sides in frying pan that is very hot. Place them in casserole large enough so that each chop will be on the bottom. On each chop place 1 tablespoon raw rice, 1 tablespoon chopped onion, a thick slice of tomato and a piece of green pepper. Sprinkle with salt, pepper, paprika and flour. Carefully pour boiling water between chops so as to disturb the mixture on each one as little as possible. Place a tight cover on casserole and bake for 3 hours in moderate oven (350°). Serve direct from the baking dish.

ROASTED STUFFED SHOULDER OF VEAL

¼ cup butter
1 large onion, chopped fine
¼ cup chopped celery
4 tablespoons chopped parsley
2 teaspoons salt
¼ teaspoon pepper

3 cups bread crumbs
1 egg
7 or 8 pound veal shoulder
  (bone removed)
  salt and pepper
2 strips lean salt pork

Melt butter in skillet and cook chopped onion in it until tender. Mix salt, celery, parsley and pepper, and add to onions. Stir in bread crumbs. Cook for 3 or 4 minutes, stirring constantly. Take up from fire, allow to cool slightly; beat egg slightly and mix into bread crumbs and seasonings.

Use stuffing to fill hole from which bone was taken. Sew up with stout button thread or light string. Sprinkle roast with salt and pepper and put in roasting pan. Lay strips of lean salt pork across roast and sear in very hot oven (500°) for 20 minutes. Then cut heat to 275° and cook 3½ hours, basting about every quarter hour. Serve with gravy.

CREAMED BAKED CHICKEN

1 cup rich milk
4 cups chicken broth
¾ cup flour
½ cup butter
½ teaspoon salt

pinch of poultry seasoning
5 cups chicken, cooked and diced
2 cups fine dry white bread
  crumbs
1 tablespoon butter
salt and pepper

In ample pot heat milk and chicken broth together. Melt butter in top of double boiler. Blend in flour, adding ½ teaspoon salt and poultry seasoning. Next blend hot liquid into this; cook until smooth and creamy and until starchy flavor of flour has disappeared. This should take about 15 minutes, with frequent stirrings. Into buttered baking dish place a layer of chicken, a layer of cream sauce and a layer of bread crumbs. Repeat until dish is full, making top layer bread crumbs. Dot with butter, sprinkle with salt and pepper, and bake uncovered in oven at 350° for about 20 to 30 minutes. This will serve ten or a dozen persons.

To prepare chicken for this dish:

Put cleaned, ready-to-cook 4½ pound stewing chicken in kettle with boiling water to cover. Add 1 teaspoon salt, 4 stalks celery, 2 onions cut up, 1 carrot, diced, and 2 peppercorns. Simmer gently for about 3 hours until tender. Remove chicken from broth and drain. Remove meat from bones and cut in generous sized pieces. Strain broth so it may be used in making gravy.

GYPSY PORK CHOPS

This was a dish Grandma prepared when she wanted to show that she too could turn out a spicy main course. Often she cooked it when the wandering Romany visitors bivouacked in our town. That's why we called it Gypsy Pork Chops.

PART I—PRUNES

½ pound large prunes
  water to cover
1 tablespoon cider vinegar

1 2-inch cinnamon stick
3 cloves
2 tablespoons brown sugar

Put prunes in saucepan, add water to cover and cook slowly until tender. Add vinegar, cinnamon stick, cloves and brown sugar. Cover and simmer gently until most of liquor is gone. Remove cloves and cinnamon stick.

PART II—PORK CHOPS

6 thick pork chops

4 tablespoons chili sauce

2 tablespoons cider vinegar

1 small onion, chopped fine

½ teaspoon dry mustard

1 teaspoon sugar

salt and pepper

Trim most of fat from chops and score lean meat with a sharp knife. Mix together chili sauce, vinegar, onion, mustard and sugar. Spread this mixture on both sides of chops. Then salt and pepper them. Let stand 1 hour so sauce can penetrate scored meat. Try out fat from chops in heavy pan and then brown chops on both sides. Cover and cook until tender. When almost done, add prunes and cook a few more minutes. Arrange chops on hot platter, remove stones from prunes and place several prunes on each chop. Then pour gravy over all and serve piping hot.

BAKED PORK CHOPS, COUNTRY STYLE

6 lean pork chops

6 medium-sized potatoes

6 medium-sized onions

6 medium-sized apples, cored, but
  not peeled

½ cup raisins

2 tablespoons brown sugar

2 cups hot beef stock (canned
  bouillon will do)

salt and pepper

Brown chops in roasting pan in hot oven (450°) for about 10 minutes. Remove roaster from oven. Arrange potatoes and onions around chops. Stuff apples with raisins, sprinkle with sugar and place an apple on top of each chop. Pour hot beef stock over all. Roast 1 hour at 375° or until vegetables are tender. Season to taste.

NEW ENGLAND BOILED DINNER

5 to 6 pounds brisket corned beef
4 whole peppercorns
8 medium-sized onions
1 white turnip, quartered
8 carrots, scraped
1 medium-sized cabbage, quartered
8 medium-sized potatoes, peeled

Have ready a large kettle. Wipe meat with damp cloth and place in kettle with peppercorns. Cover well with cold water. Bring slowly to a boil. Remove scum from water. Simmer gently for 2 to 2½ hours. At this time test for tenderness and remove peppercorns. When meat is almost done add onions, turnip and carrots. Cook 30 minutes more; then add cabbage and potatoes. Cook until potatoes are done. Serve on large platter surrounded by well-drained vegetables. Pickled beets go well with this.

CHICKEN SMOTHERED IN CREAM GRAVY

5 to 6 pound roasting chicken
½ cup flour
¼ teaspoon poultry seasoning
1 teaspoon salt
½ teaspoon pepper
½ cup butter
4 cups rich chicken broth
1 cup extra chicken broth

Cut chicken into serving pieces and wash and dry them. Mix flour and seasonings together. Dredge pieces of fowl in this seasoned flour. Melt butter in heavy pot or deep skillet. Brown a few pieces of chicken at a time. Remove to a warm pan. When last piece has been browned and removed, add whatever seasoned flour is left to drippings in pot. Mix thoroughly until smooth and slightly browned, stirring constantly. Stirring all the while, slowly add 4 cups chicken broth and cook until thickened and smooth. Place browned chicken in sauce, cover pot well and simmer very slowly over low heat until chicken is tender. Peek in occasionally lest gravy cook down too far. If this happens, add extra chicken broth. Salt and pepper if needed. Serve with hot biscuits and cranberry sauce.

MEAT LOAF

3 pounds round steak, ground	1 teaspoon black pepper
1 large onion, chopped fine	1 tablespoon tomato ketchup
1 tablespoon chopped parsley	1 egg, beaten
1 stalk celery, diced	½ cup milk
2 teaspoons salt	1 cup corn flakes

Mix ingredients, in the order given, being sure to stir well. Butter large-size loaf pan or glass baking dish and press meat into it, mounding the center a little. Bake at 350° for about 1 hour, or until well browned all over. Remove to hot platter.

DINNER-IN-A-POT

1 pound lean round steak, cut thin	3 carrots, scraped and sliced thin
½ pound sliced bacon	⅛ teaspoon salt
¼ teaspoon pepper	6 potatoes, sliced thin
3 onions, sliced	1 cup cold water

1 cup cold water

Cut steak into strips two to three inches long and about an inch wide. Cut bacon slices in half. Use heavy kettle such as you would use for chowder. Spread a layer of bacon over bottom. Then a layer of steak strips upon this. Sprinkle a little pepper over it. Next a layer of carrots and onions, sprinkled with some salt and pepper. On top place potato slices and again dust with salt and pepper. Place kettle over direct heat and after 2 minutes very gently pour water over the contents. Cover with tight-fitting lid, reduce heat at once and cook very slowly for about 40 minutes. By this time the water will be absorbed and the meat and vegetables tender and delicious.

SPRING LAMB DELIGHT

2 tablespoons shortening	1 bay leaf
2 pounds boned lamb shoulder	½ cup hot water
1 large onion, cut up	1 teaspoon sugar
1 stalk celery, cut up	½ cup cooked tomatoes
1 teaspoon salt	1 large apple, cut up and peeled
½ teaspoon pepper	½ teaspoon cornstarch

In heavy kettle, melt shortening. Add lamb which has been cut into serving pieces and brown on all sides. Add onion, celery, salt, pepper and bay leaf. Mix all together and brown lightly. Add water, sugar and tomatoes and bring to a rolling boil. Add cut-up apple. Cover and reduce heat. Simmer until lamb is tender. At this time, skim off fat and remove bay leaf. Then add cornstarch which has been dissolved in 3 tablespoons of cold water. Stir *gently* until blended. Serve with piping hot cooked rice.

FRIED MUSH

3 cups water
1 cup milk
1 tablespoon sugar

2 teaspoons salt
1 tablespoon flour
1 cup corn meal

fat for frying

Heat water and milk to boiling point in top of double boiler. Mix sugar, salt, flour, corn meal and add to water and milk, stirring constantly. Cook until thick. Then place over hot water, cover, and cook for 40 minutes, stirring once in a while. Turn out into loaf pan and chill overnight or until very firm. Cut into slices and sauté in hot fat until golden brown on both sides. Arrange on hot platter and serve with maple syrup.

PORK ROAST

1 loin roast of pork
1 tablespoon salt

1 teaspoon black pepper
3 tablespoons flour

1 large onion, sliced

Pre-heat oven to 450°. Wipe pork carefully with a clean, damp cloth. Place meat on the rack of a roaster with fat side up. Rub in salt and sprinkle pepper and flour over meat. Lay onion slices on top and place in oven, uncovered. Cook for 15 minutes, then reduce heat to 325°. Cover roaster and bake until well done, allowing 25 minutes to the pound. During the last half hour of baking remove the cover of the roaster so that the pork can become crisply browned.

WINTER PORK DISH WITH RICE

1 pound lean pork	2 cups celery, sliced in pieces
2 tablespoons melted butter	¾ teaspoon salt
½ cup onions, sliced thin	⅓ cup cold water
1½ cups hot chicken broth	2 tablespoons cornstarch
2 cups green beans, cut in pieces	1 tablespoon ketchup
2 cups carrots, sliced thin	½ teaspoon black pepper

cooked rice

Cut pork into thin strips about three inches long. In heavy kettle or large skillet place butter, pork and onions. Slowly cook until lightly browned, stirring once or twice during the process. Add chicken broth, beans, carrots, celery and salt. Cover and bring to a boil. Reduce heat and simmer for 20 minutes. Mix cold water, cornstarch, ketchup and pepper into a smooth paste. Add to mixture in kettle, stirring constantly and cooking 3 minutes longer. Serve with well-seasoned cooked rice and Aunt Annie's Chili Sauce (see page 229).

POTATO CAKES

1 cup cooked, mashed potatoes	1 tablespoon sugar
4 egg yolks, beaten	¼ teaspoon salt
1 cup flour	1 cup milk
1 teaspoon baking powder	4 egg whites, beaten stiff

Add mashed potatoes to egg yolks and beat until smooth. Sift dry ingredients and add with milk to potatoes. Stir only until mixed. Fold in egg whites. Bake on lightly greased griddle, browning well on both sides. Serve very hot with maple syrup. If thinner cakes are desired, add more milk.

CONNECTICUT BEEFSTEAK PIE

3 pounds lean rump steak   1 teaspoon salt
1 tablespoon chopped parsley   1 tablespoon cornstarch
1 teaspoon thyme   1 teaspoon Worcestershire
½ teaspoon black pepper   sauce
1 cup sliced onions   1 tablespoon fresh butter
            ¼ teaspoon grated nutmeg

Take about two cups of water and get it boiling. Then cut the steak into slices one inch thick, about three inches long and one inch wide. Cover with the boiling water. Put a lid on the pot, which should be a stout, heavy one, and allow to cook slowly for a half hour. Then add the parsley, thyme, pepper, onions and put the cover back on, cooking another half hour.

Take pot from stove. Remove one half cup of the liquor from the stew and add to it the tablespoon of cornstarch, stirring it in well until very smooth. Now stir this into the stew. Add the salt, Worcestershire sauce and butter, stirring gently. Pour it into a baking dish, sprinkle with the grated nutmeg and bake, covered, at 300° for half an hour or until hot and bubbly throughout.

The success of this dish depends upon the water being hot enough to sear the meat and keep the juices inside. Therefore if frozen meat is used it must be thoroughly defrosted and thawed so the meat will not cool down the water.

Chapter 24

Vegetable Dishes

CORN FRITTERS

2 eggs
1 cup corn cut off cob or canned
   cream-style
2½ cups flour
½ teaspoon salt

1 tablespoon sugar
1 pint milk
1 tablespoon baking powder
   vegetable shortening or lard
   for frying

Separate yolks from whites of eggs. Set whites aside. Mix together all other ingredients except shortening until well blended. Beat egg whites and fold into dough. Place heavy skillet over medium fire and melt shortening the size of a walnut. When skillet is hot, drop batter from tablespoon or mixing spoon. Brown on both sides. Serve with maple syrup and butter. Fry only enough to be eaten immediately.

COLE SLAW

2 pounds chopped cabbage	1 cup cider vinegar
2 onions, chopped fine	3 tablespoons sugar
2 carrots, shredded	1 tablespoon salt

Mix cabbage, onions and carrots in heavy bowl. Add vinegar, then sugar and salt. Mix again until all ingredients are well tossed together. Place in refrigerator to get cold.

SUGARED PARSNIPS

2 pounds parsnips	dash of ground cinnamon
½ teaspoon salt	½ cup melted butter
¼ teaspoon pepper	¼ cup flour
dash of nutmeg	1½ tablespoons sugar

butter for frying

Cook parsnips with skins on until tender. Then peel them and slice lengthwise. Season with salt, pepper and spices. Dip fully into butter and then into flour, covering each piece. Sprinkle with sugar. Fry in butter until a rich golden brown.

BAKED ACORN SQUASH

3 acorn squashes	2 tablespoons butter
2 tablespoons brown sugar	salt and pepper

Wash squashes. With a sharp knife cut them in half lengthwise. Clean out seeds and strings. Put a half inch of water into a bak-

ing dish and place the halves in it, open sides down. Bake uncovered for about 40 minutes in moderate oven (375°). Remove
from oven and turn squashes over so open sides are facing up.
Place in each hollow some brown sugar, butter and a sprinkling
of seasoning. Return to oven and bake at 375° until tender, about
15 minutes. Honey may be substituted for brown sugar by those
who prefer it.

CANNED TOMATO SALAD

1 jar home-canned tomatoes   salt and pepper
Boiled Mustard Dressing (see page 122)

Carefully remove tomatoes from jar so as not to break them.
Drain juice off and save for later use. Arrange whole tomatoes
on lettuce or plain on salad plates, season with salt and pepper,
and serve with Boiled Mustard Dressing.

In most rural New England homes salads were not too common. This tomato salad was a favorite because everyone put
up tomatoes for winter use. Lettuce was usually eaten with
sugar, salt, pepper and vinegar.

CORN OYSTERS

1 tablespoon sugar   1 teaspoon baking powder
¾ cup flour   2 eggs, well beaten
½ teaspoon salt   2 cups fresh, uncooked corn,
½ teaspoon black pepper   scraped from the cob
shortening for frying

Sift dry ingredients together and add alternately with beaten
eggs to corn. Mix well. Have ready heavy griddle or frying pan

with hot melted fat about 1 inch deep. Drop corn mixture by the tablespoonful into hot fat. Brown on one side, turn and brown on the other. These corn oysters are good served plain with main dish course or alone with maple syrup.

CORN CUSTARD

2 cups cooked corn	2 tablespoons melted butter
1 cup milk	½ teaspoon salt
3 eggs, well beaten	¼ teaspoon black pepper
3 tablespoons sugar	

Mix ingredients in the order given. Pour into buttered baking dish and bake in slow oven (325°) for 65 minutes. When a silver knife blade inserted in the center comes out clean, the custard is done. This recipe makes a full quart of custard.

SUCCOTASH

2 cups cooked lima beans	4 tablespoons butter
2 cups cooked corn	½ cup rich milk
salt and pepper to taste	

The beans and corn may be fresh, cooked or frozen but must be cooked in advance for this recipe. Lightly mix vegetables in top of double boiler. Add butter and milk. Put over boiling water and heat. Add seasonings.

ONION SHORTCAKE

2 cups onions, sliced thin	1 egg, slightly beaten
1 teaspoon salt	½ cup sour cream
2 tablespoons butter	¼ teaspoon black pepper
biscuit dough (see page 161)	

Cook onions with salt and butter in saucepan in enough water to cover. When almost tender but *not* browned, remove from fire and cool. Put a round of biscuit dough about ½ inch thick in greased baking dish. Beat egg and cream and pepper together. Place onions on top of dough and pour cream mixture over all. Bake uncovered in hot oven (425°) for 20 minutes.

OLD-STYLE SCALLOPED POTATOES

6 medium-sized potatoes, sliced thin	2 tablespoons flour
3 onions, sliced thin	1 teaspoon salt
3 stalks celery, sliced	½ teaspoon black pepper
2 tablespoons chopped green parsley	7 tablespoons butter
	2¼ cups hot milk

Butter a baking dish. Place in it a layer each of potatoes, onions and celery. Add a little parsley. Sprinkle with flour, salt and pepper and dot with butter. Continue until all vegetables are used up. Pour hot milk over all. Cover and bake in slow oven (325°) for 1 hour, or until potatoes are tender. If dish becomes dry, add more milk.

Grandma liked to fix this dish at the same time she baked a meat loaf as neither one required watching and she could do some of her other "chores" while they cooked. They went together like bride and groom, too.

SPRING GREENS

This was a dish that followed the first dose of sulphur and molasses in the spring. No exact recipe is possible.

Pick whatever new greens are available: dandelions, cowslips, young beet tops, turnip greens or chard. Wash and remove roots and dead leaves. Carefully sort out brown leaves, as these will be bitter. Cook in a small amount of boiling water, to which a dash of salt has been added. When tender add 1 tablespoon cider vinegar, 1 teaspoon sugar, ¼ teaspoon black pepper and 2 tablespoons butter. Toss gently with a fork before serving.

GARDEN LETTUCE, YANKEE STYLE

1 head Boston lettuce	1 tablespoon sugar
2 slices bacon	½ teaspoon salt
1 tablespoon cider vinegar	¼ teaspoon pepper
1 teaspoon onion juice	

Pick lettuce leaves over, wash and dry. Dice bacon and cook in skillet until crisp. Quickly add to this vinegar, sugar, salt and pepper and allow to boil up *once*. Remove from heat, add onion juice, pour all over lettuce and toss gently but thoroughly.

BAKED LIMA BEANS

½ cup chopped salt pork	2 cups lima beans, fresh
½ cup onions, chopped very fine	2 cups boiling water
1 cup carrots, scraped and diced	2 tablespoons butter
salt and pepper to taste	

Cook salt pork in heavy pan for 5 minutes. Add onion, and brown. Add carrots and beans. Pour into baking dish and add water. Dot with butter. Cover and bake about an hour at 325° until tender.

AUNT ANNIE'S RED POTATO SALAD

1½ cups cooked potatoes, diced
2 cups cooked beets, diced
½ cup tender celery, diced
3 hard-boiled eggs, chopped up
½ cup cooked green peas
2 tablespoons chopped green
  parsley

1 teaspoon salt
½ teaspoon pepper
¾ cup boiled mustard
  dressing
1 hard-boiled egg, sliced to
  garnish
Hungarian paprika

extra Boiled Mustard Dressing

Toss together potatoes, beets, celery, chopped eggs, peas, parsley, seasonings and ¾ cup of Grandma's Boiled Mustard Dressing (page 122). Pile lightly on garden lettuce or in serving dish. Garnish with slices of hard-boiled egg and sprinkle with paprika. Have extra dressing handy for passing.

Chapter 25

Bread and Rolls

GRANDMA'S OWN WHITE BREAD

2 cakes yeast
1 cup lukewarm milk
2 tablespoons sugar
1 tablespoon salt

2 tablespoons butter
2 cups scalding milk
2 eggs, beaten
6 to 6½ cups sifted flour

melted butter

Soften yeast in lukewarm milk. Put in large mixing bowl sugar, salt and butter. Pour scalding milk over this and allow to cool down until lukewarm. Add yeast mixture and eggs.

152

Beat well. Mix in with spoon 2 cups flour. Then beat well again. Then add enough flour to make a dough that pulls away from side of bowl. Beat until smooth and until no dry flour is noticeable. Cover with wax paper and clean towel. Let rise in warm place until double in bulk. (This takes about 1½ hours.)

Put out dough on lightly floured board and knead *thoroughly*. Divide into 2 parts. Mold each into a loaf, kneading dough to get out bubbles and to make smooth and light. Roll into loaf shapes and place in buttered bread pans. Dough should fill pans about ⅔ full. Cover with wax paper and towel. Let rise in warm place until sides of dough reach tops of pans and centers are well rounded above this point. Bake at 425° for 10 minutes. Then reduce heat to 350° and finish baking for 35 minutes. Remove from pans to cake racks. Brush with melted butter.

ANNADAMA BREAD

½ cup water-ground corn meal	3 teaspoons salt
2 cups boiling water	2 cakes yeast
2 tablespoons butter	½ cup lukewarm water
½ cup molasses	7 to 8 cups sifted white flour
melted butter	

While stirring constantly, add corn meal to boiling water. Add to this butter, molasses and salt, and cool down to lukewarm (about 85°). Break yeast into lukewarm water and let stand until first mixture is cool. Then stir yeast into corn-meal mixture. Add enough flour to make a rather stiff dough. Put out on floured board and knead well. Then place in buttered bowl, cover with wax paper and clean towel. Allow to rise in warm place until double in bulk. Put out on floured board and knead well. Add more flour if necessary. Shape into 2 loaves and place in greased loaf pans. Cover again and allow to rise until nearly double, or until dough has reached the shape of desired loaf. Bake at 425° for 10 minutes. Then cut heat down to 350° and bake for 50 minutes. Remove bread at once and place on cake racks. Brush crust with butter.

SOUR CREAM ROLLS

2 cups sour cream	2 teaspoons salt
1 cake yeast	¼ teaspoon baking soda
¼ cup lukewarm water	5 cups flour (approximate)
3 tablespoons sugar	melted butter

Scald the cream. Crumble yeast into lukewarm water. Put sugar, salt and baking soda into large bowl and pour scalded cream over them. Cool to lukewarm. Add yeast and half the flour. Beat well. Add enough flour to make a soft dough. Turn onto lightly floured board and knead until smooth and springy. Roll out. Cut into desired shapes. Brush with melted butter. Place on greased baking sheets. Cover with wax paper or damp towel. Allow to rise until double in bulk. Bake in hot oven (425°) for 15 minutes. This should make from 4 to 5 dozen rolls depending on size.

HOT CROSS BUNS

⅔ cup scalded milk	3 eggs, beaten
2 cakes yeast	2½ cups flour
⅓ cup sugar	⅔ cup currants
1 cup flour	½ teaspoon cinnamon
½ cup melted butter	1 egg white, lightly beaten
¾ teaspoon salt	¾ cup powdered sugar

Allow scalded milk to become lukewarm. Soften yeast in it and then add sugar. Take 1 cup flour and add to mixture, beating it well. Then add butter, salt, eggs and 2½ cups flour. Beat until dough is light. Cover with wax paper and clean towel and allow to rise in warm place until double in bulk. Then add currants and cinnamon and mix well. Roll out on lightly floured board until about a half inch thick. Cut with a sharp knife and shape into buns. Place on greased cookie sheet. Again allow to rise until double in bulk. Brush each bun with lightly beaten egg white and bake in moderate oven (350°) for 15 minutes.

Make frosting by adding powdered sugar to remaining egg white. Using a small spoon or a pastry tube, fashion a cross with the frosting on each bun.

THIN INDIAN BREAD

2 cups water-ground corn meal
1 tablespoon butter
1 teaspoon salt

boiling water
1 cup cold milk
2 eggs, well beaten

Mix together corn meal, butter and salt. Scald with boiling water to consistency of thick mush. Mix well. Thin down with cold milk and eggs. Spread thin on buttered baking pan. Bake until brown in moderate oven (350°). Serve hot.

AUNT KAY'S POTATO BREAD AND COFFEE RING

½ cup butter
½ cup sugar
3 eggs
2 cakes yeast

½ cup lukewarm potato water
1 cup riced potato
1 teaspoon salt
1 cup milk

8 cups flour (approximate)

Cream butter and sugar. Beat in eggs, one at a time. Dissolve yeast in water in which potatoes were cooked. Add with riced potato to the first mixture and beat well. Add salt, milk and half the flour. Beat until smooth. Then add enough flour to make a stiff dough. Mix well, cover and let rise until double in bulk. Turn out on a floured board.

For the Bread: Take ⅔ of dough and knead well. Divide in half. Knead and shape each half into a loaf. Put into 2 greased bread pans, cover and let rise in warm place until nicely rounded up. This takes about 1 hour. Bake for 50 minutes at 375°. Brush crust with melted butter and cool on racks.

For the Coffee Ring: Knead remaining dough until light and smooth. Roll into an oblong sheet and spread with 3 tablespoons soft butter, ½ cup sugar, 2 tablespoons cinnamon and ¾ cup seedless raisins. Roll like a jelly roll. Form into a ring on a greased baking sheet. Cut slashes through top of ring, only part way through, at 2-inch intervals. Cover and let rise until double in bulk. Bake at 375° for 30 minutes.

CRANBERRY MUFFINS

¼ cup butter
¼ cup brown sugar
1 egg, beaten
2 cups sifted flour
3 teaspoons baking powder

½ teaspoon salt
1 cup milk
1 cup raw cranberries, chopped fine
1 teaspoon orange flavoring

Cream together butter, sugar and egg. Sift dry ingredients together. Add alternately with milk to butter mixture, beating just enough to dampen all ingredients. Fold in cranberries and flavoring. Fill greased muffin tins ⅔ full. Bake in hot oven (400°) for 25 minutes, or until lightly browned. Muffins should have slightly rounded tops. Peaked muffins are the result of too much beating. Makes 12 average-sized muffins.

RAISIN BREAD

1 box seedless raisins	1 teaspoon salt
2 cakes yeast	1 teaspoon cinnamon
¼ cup lukewarm water	⅛ teaspoon mace
2 cups milk	1 teaspoon lemon extract
2 tablespoons butter	2 eggs, beaten
2 tablespoons sugar	6 cups flour (approx.)

Soak raisins 1 hour in 2 cups cold water and drain. Dissolve yeast in lukewarm water. Scald milk. Put butter, sugar, salt, spices and flavoring in large mixing bowl. Pour scalded milk over all. When mixture is lukewarm add eggs and dissolved yeast. Mix in half the flour, beating thoroughly until smooth. Add remaining flour to make a stiff dough. Put out on floured board and knead until springy. Place in large greased bowl, cover and let rise in warm place until double in bulk. Remove to floured board, knead again and divide into 2 parts. Knead and shape into 2 loaves, put in greased bread pans, and let rise until double in bulk. Bake 15 minutes at 400°; reduce heat and bake at 350° for 35 minutes. Brush with melted butter and remove to racks to cool.

OATMEAL BREAD

1 cup regular rolled oats	½ cup molasses
2 tablespoons butter	2 cakes yeast
2 cups boiling water	½ cup lukewarm water
2 teaspoons salt	5 cups flour

Soak oats and butter in boiling water for 1 hour. When cool, add salt and molasses. Beat well. Add yeast which has been softened in lukewarm water. Then add flour, mixing well. Cover and let rise in warm place until double in bulk. Put out on lightly floured board. Knead and pummel dough until light and springy. Shape into 2 loaves. Put into well-greased pans. Let rise until dough comes to edges of bread tins and centers are nicely rounded. Bake at 350° for 1 hour, or until the crust gives a "ping" when tapped smartly with thumbnail. Brush crusts with melted butter and cool on cake racks.

HUCKLEBERRY GRIDDLE CAKES

2 cups flour	1½ cups milk
½ teaspoon salt	2 eggs, well beaten
4 teaspoons baking powder	3 tablespoons melted butter
2 tablespoons sugar	1 cup fresh huckleberries

fat for frying

Sift dry ingredients together. Quickly mix in milk, eggs and melted butter. Beat until light. Fold in the huckleberries. Drop batter onto lightly greased hot griddle. Brown on one side thoroughly. When tops are full of bubbles and edges brown, turn cakes, and brown on other side. Serve at once with maple syrup and butter.

STEAMED BROWN BREAD

1 cup rye meal	2 teaspoons baking soda
1 cup corn meal	2 teaspoons cream of tartar
½ cup graham flour	½ cup molasses
½ cup white flour	2 cups sour milk
½ teaspoon salt	1 cup raisins

Mix dry ingredients thoroughly. Put molasses and sour milk in large mixing bowl. Add mixed dry ingredients and beat well. Put into well-buttered molds and steam for 3 hours. Remove from molds. If eaten hot, cut the slices with a string.

HUCKLEBERRY MUFFINS

In Grandma's day huckleberries were found growing wild in upland pastures and burned over woodlots. Today they are harder to find. Domestic blueberries are sold everywhere now, though, and can be used with excellent results wherever one of Grandma's recipes calls for huckleberries.

2 cups sifted flour	1 cup milk
2 teaspoons baking powder	1 large egg, beaten
4 tablespoons sugar	3 tablespoons melted butter
½ teaspoon salt	1½ cups fresh huckleberries

Sift dry ingredients in mixing bowl. Quickly mix in milk, egg and butter. Gently fold in the berries. Fill greased muffin tins only ⅔ full. Bake in hot oven (400°) for 20 minutes.

MOLASSES AND APPLE MUFFINS

2 cups sifted flour	¼ cup melted butter
1 teaspoon cinnamon	¾ cup molasses
¼ teaspoon ginger	1 egg, well beaten
¼ teaspoon nutmeg	1 tablespoon milk
½ teaspoon salt	¼ cup currants, washed and
1 teaspoon baking soda	drained
3 tablespoons dark brown sugar	2 apples, peeled and cut into
	eighths

Sift dry ingredients together in large mixing bowl. Add butter and molasses and mix well. Stir in egg and milk. Add currants. Arrange apple slices in bottom of greased muffin tins. Spoon muffin mixture over apples. Bake at 350° for 25 minutes. Serve hot, but muffins are also good cold if any are left over.

OATMEAL MUFFINS

2 cups regular rolled oats
1½ cups milk
¼ cup melted butter
⅓ cup dark brown sugar
½ teaspoon salt

1 egg, beaten
¾ cup seedless raisins, washed
   and drained
1 cup sifted flour
3 teaspoons baking powder

Put oats in mixing bowl. Scald milk and pour hot over oats. Cool. Add butter, sugar, salt and egg. Add raisins. Mix well. Sift flour with baking powder. Add quickly to mixture. Put into greased muffin tins, filling about ⅔ full, and bake at 375° for 20 minutes. Makes 12 to 16 muffins.

OLD-TIME CORN BREAD

1 cup water-ground white corn
   meal
1 cup sifted flour
½ teaspoon salt

¾ cup dark brown sugar
½ teaspoon baking soda
1 egg, well beaten
½ cup sour milk

⅓ cup sour cream

Sift dry ingredients together. Add liquid ingredients. Beat well, but quickly. Pour into greased baking pan. Bake for 20 minutes in very hot oven (450°).

BUTTERMILK BISCUITS

2 cups sifted flour
2 teaspoons baking powder
¼ teaspoon baking soda

1 teaspoon salt ¾ t salt
5 tablespoons butter
¾ cup buttermilk

Sift dry ingredients together. Work in butter with fork or fingers until finely mixed. Stir in buttermilk to make a soft dough. Put out on lightly floured board and knead slightly, just enough to shine up dough. Pat out to 1 inch thickness. Cut desired rounds with lightly floured cutter. Place closely together in lightly greased baking pan. Bake in hot oven (475°) for 10 minutes, or until as brown as desired. This makes a high, fluffy type of biscuit and was one of Grandma's favorites.

PRUNE BUNS

2 cups sifted flour
4 teaspoons baking powder
2 tablespoons sugar
½ teaspoon salt
2 tablespoons shortening

1 egg, well beaten
¾ cup milk
12 to 15 stewed prunes, pitted
1½ teaspoons lemon juice
12 teaspoons sugar

2 teaspoons cinnamon

Sift together flour, baking powder, 2 tablespoons sugar and salt. Add shortening and mix in with fork or fingers. Add egg and milk to make a soft dough. Roll this dough thinner than for ordinary biscuits. Cut in 3-inch squares (12 or 15) and on each square place a prune, a bit of lemon juice, 1 teaspoon sugar and a sprinkling of cinnamon. Fold over and press edges together. Bake in hot oven (450°) for 12 minutes. Ice each bun with a simple confectioner's frosting made of confectioner's sugar and water and flavored with lemon. Delicious hot, but fine cold.

HUCKLEBERRY CORN CAKE

1 cup corn meal	1 large egg, beaten
1 cup flour	1 full cup cleaned huckle-
¼ cup sugar	berries
¾ teaspoon salt	1 cup milk
5 teaspoons baking powder	2 tablespoons melted butter

Sift dry ingredients together and then add berries. Add milk and butter to egg. Combine mixtures, stirring only until all is dampened. Put into shallow greased pan and bake at 425° for 25 minutes. This batter may also be baked in greased muffin tins.

ROLLED CINNAMON LOAF

2 cakes yeast	1 teaspoon lemon flavoring
3 tablespoons lukewarm water	4 cups flour
⅓ cup white sugar	1 tablespoon softened butter
¾ teaspoon salt	⅓ cup dark brown sugar
¼ cup butter	2 teaspoons cinnamon
1 cup scalded milk	½ cup seedless raisins
1 egg, well beaten	melted butter

Soften yeast in lukewarm water. Put sugar, salt and butter in large mixing bowl. Pour scalded milk over this and stir. Cool to lukewarm. Add yeast, egg and flavoring. Beat well. Add flour to this, beating until springy and well mixed. Put out onto well floured board. Knead until light and springy. Roll to ¼ inch thickness in an oblong shape and spread with softened butter. Sprinkle with brown sugar and cinnamon and scatter raisins over all. Roll up tightly as for a jelly roll. Put into well-greased bread pan. Let rise until double in bulk. Bake at 375° for 1 hour. Cool on rack after brushing crust with melted butter. It is delicious eaten hot out of the oven, too.

CORN MEAL DUMPLINGS

1 teaspoon salt
1 cup corn meal
1⅓ cups boiling water
1 teaspoon finely chopped onion
1 teaspoon finely chopped
   parsley

¼ teaspoon nutmeg
¼ teaspoon black pepper
2 eggs, beaten
flour sufficient for dredging

Add salt to corn meal and pour boiling water over it, stirring constantly all the while. Stir until it forms a smooth, thick mush. Cool. Add onion, parsley, seasonings and eggs. Mix well and form into desired sized dumplings. Roll each one in flour and drop on top of any stew while latter is boiling. Cover tightly. Steam 10 to 15 minutes.

RAISED BUCKWHEAT GRIDDLE CAKES

To make these the cook must know she wants them the night before as the batter must be set at night.

1 cake yeast
3 cups lukewarm water
1 teaspoon salt
2 tablespoons sugar

2 cups buckwheat flour
1 cup white flour
2 tablespoons molasses
2 tablespoons butter, melted

½ teaspoon baking soda

At night, soften yeast in lukewarm water. Sift together salt, sugar, buckwheat and white flours and stir into yeast mixture, beating until well blended. Cover and place in warm place away from draughts. In the morning, add molasses, butter and soda, stirring them in quickly but thoroughly. Bake on hot greased griddle. These griddle cakes are excellent with the usual bacon and eggs, ham or sausage, and are delicious with maple syrup or with the thick syrup left from home-canned peaches.

HOLYPOKES

These delicacies are made with bread dough for which the recipe is given on page 152. Normally a cook divides the recipe and makes one loaf of bread or a batch of rolls and uses the balance of the dough for the holypokes.

To make the holypokes let the dough rise once and then put out on a floured board. Knead. Form into balls the size of hazelnuts or walnuts. Place on a buttered cookie sheet, cover with waxed paper and dampened tea towel. Let rise in a warm place until they are doubled in size.

Heat a kettle of fat to 360°. Drop the holypokes into the deep fat and cook until they become a golden brown. Drain on absorbent paper. Serve with butter as companions to soups and chowders or serve with maple syrup as a dessert.

Chapter 26

Desserts and Pies

PASTRY FOR ONE-CRUST PIE

1¼ cups flour
½ teaspoon salt

7 tablespoons shortening
3 to 4 tablespoons cold water

Sift flour and salt together twice. Add shortening and cut it in until particles are the size of peas. Gradually sprinkle cold water over mixture. Work lightly together with fork or fingers until dough is formed. Roll dough on lightly floured board to about ⅛ inch thickness. Place in pie pan. Pat *gently* and loosely into shape of pan. Trim 1 inch larger than pan and turn back to form fluted edge. *If* pastry is to be baked before filling, prick all over with fork. Then bake at 450° for 12 minutes. Handle gently. If to be used unbaked, refrigerate until needed.

PASTRY FOR TWO-CRUST PIE

⅔ cup shortening	1 teaspoon salt
2 cups flour	6 to 8 tablespoons water

Add shortening to flour and salt. Mix in lightly with fingers or fork until coarse—about like rolled oats. Add half of water, mixing gently. Then add more water until flour is just damp. Turn out on floured board and form into a ball. Divide in half. Roll each half separately to form the 2 crusts.

PEACH COBBLER

1 egg	½ teaspoon salt
½ cup sugar	8 large peaches, peeled and
3 tablespoons melted butter	sliced
⅓ cup milk	⅔ cup sugar
½ cup flour	¼ teaspoon nutmeg
2 teaspoons baking powder	¼ teaspoon cinnamon

Beat egg, add ½ cup sugar, butter and milk. Sift flour, baking powder and salt together and add to egg mixture. Beat thoroughly.

Fill large buttered baking dish about halfway with peaches which have been mixed with ⅔ cup sugar and spices. Cover with batter mixture, spreading latter smoothly. Bake at 375° for 30 minutes. Serve hot with cream or Grandma's Pudding Sauce.

GRANDMA'S PUDDING SAUCE

1 tablespoon cornstarch   1 cup boiling water
½ cup sugar   1½ tablespoons butter
  pinch of salt   1½ teaspoons lemon flavoring
       1½ teaspoons vanilla flavoring

Combine cornstarch, sugar, salt, and mix well. Add boiling water, stirring constantly, and boil *gently* for 5 minutes. Add butter and flavorings. Serve hot. Makes 1¼ cups sauce. Guaranteed mouth-watering.

UPSIDE-DOWN APPLE PIE

6 large tart apples, pared and   ¼ teaspoon nutmeg
  sliced thin   ½ teaspoon cinnamon
½ cup washed seeded raisins   2 tablespoons butter
¾ cup light brown sugar   1 unbaked pastry top (use
2 tablespoons flour   recipe for pastry for 1-crust
½ teaspoon lemon flavoring   pie, see p. 165)

Blend dry ingredients together. Mix with apples, raisins and flavorings. Fill buttered pie pan, rounding full with mixture. Dot with butter. Cover with pastry top to the edges. Slit pastry cover with sharp knife. Bake at 450° for 10 minutes. Then bake at 350° for 30 minutes until apples are tender. Serve upside-down with cream, or Grandma's Pudding Sauce (see page 167).

ORANGE SHORTCAKE

2 cups flour   ⅓ cup butter
4 teaspoons baking powder   1 egg, well beaten
1 tablespoon sugar   ½ cup milk
½ teaspoon salt   1 teaspoon melted butter
       3 cups fresh orange sections

Sift dry ingredients together in mixing bowl. Cut in butter with fork and fingers. Add egg and milk, stirring only until dry ingredients are dampened. Put out on lightly floured board and divide in half. Roll out each half the size of a layer cake. Place one section in layer cake pan, brush with melted butter and then top with second half. Bake at 425° for 25 minutes. Remove to serving platter, lift off top layer and cover bottom layer with some of the orange sections, which have been carefully seeded and freed from their membranes. Place top layer on shortcake and pile remaining oranges and juice over all. Serve warm with cream.

AUNT LYDIA'S CREAM PIE

2 cups milk
½ cup sugar
2 egg yolks, beaten
2 heaping tablespoons cornstarch
1 teaspoon vanilla flavoring

1 teaspoon lemon flavoring
¼ teaspoon nutmeg
1 baked pastry shell (see page 165)
2 tablespoons fine sugar

2 egg whites, beaten stiff

Place milk and sugar in saucepan, bring to a near boil. Beat egg yolks and cornstarch until smooth. Add slowly to milk and sugar mixture. Cook over low heat, stirring constantly, until thickened. Add flavorings. Pour into pastry shell. Cover with meringue made by gently folding sugar with egg whites. Put into oven and bake at 325° until meringue is lightly browned.

MOLASSES PRUNE PIE

½ pound dried prunes
½ cup prune juice
¼ cup sugar
¾ cup molasses
4 egg yolks, beaten

¼ cup home-made preserves
¼ cup melted butter
1 teaspoon vinegar or lemon juice
pastry for 1-crust pie (see page 165)

Wash prunes and cover with cold water. Soak overnight or equivalent time. Cook slowly until tender. Drain, saving juice. Mix together ½ cup prune juice, sugar, molasses and egg yolks. Cut prunes into small pieces, discarding pits. Mix preserves— which can be apple, orange, peach or Damson plum—with prunes, butter and flavoring. Add to egg mixture. Place in pastry-lined pan. Cover with strips of rolled pastry to please own taste and bake at 450° for 10 minutes. Then bake at 350° for 30 minutes, until firm. Cool and serve.

POOR MAN'S RASPBERRY PIE

1½ cups raisins
1½ cups sweetened raspberry
   juice

1½ tablespoons cornstarch
4 tablespoons cold raspberry
   juice

pastry for 2-crust pie (see page 166)

Boil raisins in 1½ cups raspberry juice for 3 minutes. Blend cornstarch and 4 tablespoons cold raspberry juice. Add to first mixture. Cook until clear, stirring constantly. Pour into pastry-lined pan and cover with slitted top crust. Bake at 400° for 30 minutes.

This recipe uses up the juice often left over from home canning of raspberries. Juice from canned or frozen berries may be substituted. The pie tastes so much like real raspberry pie few can tell the difference. That explains the name.

BUTTERMILK PIE

½ cup butter
⅔ cup sugar
3 egg yolks
3 tablespoons flour
½ teaspoon salt

grated rind of 1 lemon
1 tablespoon lemon juice
2 cups buttermilk
3 egg whites
1 10-inch baked pastry shell
   (see page 165)

Cream butter. Slowly add sugar while creaming. Add egg yolks one at a time, beating thoroughly after each one. Add flour, salt, lemon rind and lemon juice. Mix well. Add buttermilk, beating it in. Beat egg whites until stiff but not dry. Fold carefully into buttermilk mixture. Pour into baked pastry shell. Bake at 375° for 45 minutes.

HOT HUCKLEBERRY CAKE WITH SAUCE

½ cup sugar	1 teaspoon ground cloves
½ cup butter	1 teaspoon grated nutmeg
1 cup dark molasses	1 teaspoon ginger
1 egg	2½ cups sifted flour
1 tablespoon soda	1 cup boiling water
1 teaspoon salt	1 cup huckleberries

Cream sugar and butter together. Stir in molasses and beat in egg. Sift dry ingredients together. Beat them into first mixture; then slowly add boiling water. Beat thoroughly. Fold in huckleberries. Pour into greased, floured 9-inch pan and bake at 350° for 40 minutes. Serve hot with Huckleberry Sauce.

HUCKLEBERRY SAUCE

Put into saucepan 1 pint huckleberries, 1 cup water, ½ cup sugar, 1 teaspoon cider vinegar and ½ teaspoon cinnamon. Bring to a full boil. Blend 2 tablespoons cornstarch with ¼ cup cold water. Add slowly to huckleberry mixture. Cook until clear.

CARAMEL PIE

This recipe makes two pies. They are so rich and festive-looking that Grandma always made two and sent one to a neighbor.

1 cup butter
2 cups dark brown sugar
5 egg yolks, beaten
1 cup preserves

1 teaspoon vanilla flavoring
¼ teaspoon salt
5 egg whites, beaten
2 baked pastry shells (see page 166)

Cream butter and sugar until light. Then stir in egg yolks, preserves, vanilla and salt. Carefully fold in beaten egg whites. Divide between 2 baked pastry shells. Bake in slow oven (300-325°) for 45 minutes.

SOUR CREAM RAISIN PIE

4 eggs
1 cup sugar
½ teaspoon salt
2 cups raisins

2 cups sour cream
1 unbaked pastry shell (see page 165)
2 egg whites

2 tablespoons sugar

Beat eggs lightly. Add sugar, salt, raisins and cream. Mix thoroughly and pour into unbaked shell. Bake in hot oven (400°) for 10 minutes. Lower temperature to 350° and bake 20 minutes longer, or until custard is firm. Remove from oven and cover with meringue made by beating 2 egg whites until stiff and slowly adding 2 tablespoons sugar. Return to oven until meringue is lightly browned.

OLD-FASHIONED RICE PUDDING

2 tablespoons raw rice
1 quart rich milk
¼ cup sugar
¼ teaspoon salt

½ cup raisins
1 teaspoon vanilla flavoring
¼ teaspoon nutmeg
¼ teaspoon cinnamon

Wash and drain rice. Mix remaining ingredients together in buttered baking dish. Bake in slow oven (275°) for from 2 to 3 hours, until pudding is firm and lightly browned. Stir occasionally during first hour.

STEAMED CRANBERRY PUDDING

1 cup flour	⅓ cup brown sugar
2 teaspoons baking powder	2 tablespoons white sugar
½ teaspoon salt	⅔ cup finely chopped suet
½ cup soft bread crumbs	1 cup chopped cranberries

⅓ cup milk

Mix ingredients in the order given. Pour into greased mold. Steam for 2 hours. This pudding is best if served hot with Grandma's Pudding Sauce (see page 167).

This pudding is still the favorite in eastern Massachusetts, where the berries grow abundantly in the low bogs.

FARMER'S DELIGHT

1 pint huckleberries	powdered sugar
1 tablespoon cornstarch	1 layer of sponge cake (see
juice of ½ lemon	next page)
pinch of salt	whipped or heavy cream
¼ cup water	nutmeg to taste

Into heavy saucepan place huckleberries, cornstarch, sugar, lemon juice, salt and water. Stir gently until well mixed. Then cook, stirring carefully, until thickened. Put this aside to cool. Slice layer of cake to make two layers. Put some of the berries into pudding dish and cover with one layer of cake. Place more berries on top. Then add second layer of cake. Put remaining berries on this layer. Sprinkle powdered sugar generously over all and then cut cake into wedge-shaped serving portions. Whipped cream, or plain thick cream, is excellent if used as topping for each portion. Dust whipped cream with a little nutmeg and add a few fresh huckleberries for color.

SPONGE CAKE

6 egg yolks	6 egg whites, beaten stiff
1 cup granulated sugar	1 cup sifted flour
1½ tablespoons lemon juice	½ teaspoon salt

Beat egg yolks until they become thick and lemon colored. Gradually add sugar, continuing beating, and then lemon juice. Beat this well. Fold in stiffly beaten egg whites and then fold in sifted flour and salt. Pour batter into ungreased tube pan or into 2 ungreased layer pans. Bake in slow oven (325°). The batter in the tube pan should require 50 minutes and the batter in the layer pans will need 40 minutes.

The cake will be done when the center springs back when lightly pressed with fingertip. Remove from the oven and invert the pan. Let it cool. Then run a knife around the center tube and sides of the tube pan and the sides of the layer pans and work the cake easily out of the containers. When cutting sponge cake use two forks or an exceedingly sharp knife to avoid mashing the cake and hurting the airy texture.

LEMON SPONGE PUDDING

2 tablespoons butter	2 tablespoons flour
¾ cup sugar	juice of 1 lemon
2 eggs, separated	grated rind of ½ lemon
1 cup milk	

Cream butter, adding sugar gradually and continuing to work mixture until all is creamed together well. Add well-beaten egg yolks, flour, lemon juice and lemon rind. Mix thoroughly. Add milk and fold in egg whites which have been stiffly beaten. Pour mixture into greased baking dish. Set this in pan of hot water and bake at 350° for 45 minutes. A delicate brown crust will be formed on the top as the lighter ingredients tend to float to the top. This pudding is delicious hot or chilled.

APPLE FOAM

2 cups cold applesauce   1 egg white, stiffly beaten
½ teaspoon cinnamon   ½ cup whipped cream
                    ½ teaspoon nutmeg

This is a quick dessert. Just before serving fold into applesauce, which has been sweetened to taste, cinnamon, egg white and cream. Both egg white and cream should have been beaten very stiff. Grandma sprinkled nutmeg over the top as a garnish and served this dessert on days when she didn't have time to prepare a cooked dish.

DRIED APPLE CUSTARD

3 cups dried apples   ½ cup melted butter
   cold water to cover   ¼ teaspoon salt
¾ cup white sugar   1 teaspoon lemon flavoring
¼ cup brown sugar   1 teaspoon vanilla flavoring
   6 egg yolks, well beaten   6 egg whites, beaten stiff

Soak dried apples overnight in water to cover. Then cook for 20 minutes as though they were fresh apples. Add more water if needed. Sweeten resulting sauce with white and brown sugars and whip until it is very smooth. Add 2 cups of this sauce to egg yolks along with melted butter and salt. Mix thoroughly. Cook in top of double boiler over gently boiling water until thick and creamy. Remove from fire and add flavorings. Then fold in stiffly beaten egg whites. Dried apples give this dessert a taste that cannot be obtained by using fresh ones.

SATIN PUDDING

1 cup sugar	5 egg yolks, well beaten
1 quart milk	⅛ teaspoon salt
3 tablespoons cornstarch	1½ teaspoons vanilla flavoring
½ cup cold milk	5 egg whites, beaten stiff
5 tablespoons sugar	

Put sugar into milk in top of double boiler. Bring this *almost* to a boil. Dissolve cornstarch in cold milk and blend into egg yolks. Stir this *very* slowly into hot milk mixture. Cook, stirring constantly, until it resembles very heavy cream. Remove from fire, add salt and flavoring and pour into very lightly buttered baking dish. Make meringue by beating egg whites stiffly and gradually adding 5 tablespoons sugar. Cover pudding with this meringue and bake in oven registering 350° until meringue is a light golden brown. Serve this pudding very cold.

PEACH FRITTERS WITH SAUCE

3½ cups sliced peaches	¼ teaspoon salt
1 cup flour	⅓ cup milk
1½ teaspoons baking powder	1 large egg, beaten
3 tablespoons sugar	shortening for frying
2 tablespoons powdered sugar	

The peaches for this dessert may be fresh, cooked, or canned. In any event, save syrup for sauce. Mix flour, baking powder, sugar and salt together and sift several times. Add milk and egg. Beat until smooth and light. Dip peach slices in this batter and fry in shallow fat (1½ inches deep) at about 375° until lightly browned. Drain and sprinkle with powdered sugar. These fritters are best when served with Peach Sauce.

PEACH SAUCE

½ cup sugar
1 tablespoon cornstarch
⅛ teaspoon salt
1 cup peach syrup

¼ cup seedless raisins
1 egg yolk, lightly beaten
2 tablespoons butter
3 tablespoons lemon juice

Mix together sugar, cornstarch and salt. Bring syrup to a boil on top of stove. Slowly add it to cornstarch mixture, stirring until smooth. Add raisins. Cook over hot water for 15 minutes. Pour cornstarch mixture on egg yolk and mix well. Add butter and lemon juice. Serve hot on Peach Fritters.

FRESH CHERRY PUDDING

2 cups ripe seeded cherries
sugar
¾ cup sugar
1 teaspoon salt

2½ cups flour
2 teaspoons baking powder
1 cup milk
1 egg, beaten

3 tablespoons melted butter

When seeding ripe cherries add a little sugar to gain the precise degree of sweetness desired. When fruit is seeded, mix ¾ cup sugar and salt with cherries. Place in bottom of buttered baking dish. Next, mix and sift dry ingredients together. Add milk and beaten egg to butter and blend thoroughly. Pour this batter over cherries. Bake 40 minutes at 350°. This pudding can be served from the dish, hot or cold, with Grandma's Sauce (see page 167) or whipped cream. It can also be turned out of the baking dish on a suitable, deep-edged serving dish which leaves the cherries on top. The sauce or cream will add a satin taste the pudding itself does not possess.

OLD-FASHIONED BOILED CUSTARD

Grandma used this custard in many ways—with cake, cookies, fruit or puddings, or by itself. She usually had some on hand in a covered jar and its addition made simple dishes seem luxurious.

1 tablespoon cornstarch	4 tablespoons sugar
4 cups milk	½ teaspoon salt
4 eggs	1½ teaspoons vanilla flavoring

Dissolve cornstarch in a little cold milk. Bring remainder of milk to a boil. Add cornstarch. Smooth it in and cook *slowly* for 10 minutes. Beat eggs and sugar and salt together and pour boiling milk over mixture. Blend all together and return to stove. Cook slowly until thick enough to mask spoon. Take off heat at once. Set in pan of cold water and stir often so as to cool custard down quickly. Then add flavoring. Pour into serving dishes if eaten at once, or into jars for refrigeration.

BAKED CUSTARD AND CHOCOLATE CUSTARD

6 eggs	1 teaspoon vanilla flavoring
½ cup sugar	4 cups milk
½ teaspoon salt	¼ teaspoon nutmeg

Beat eggs slightly. Add sugar, salt, flavoring and milk. Pour into individual baking dishes or into 1 large baking dish. Sprinkle with nutmeg. Set in pan of hot water. Bake at 325° for 50 minutes if using single large dish, for 40 minutes if using small ones, or until a silver knife blade inserted into custard comes out smooth and clean, with no custard adhering to blade. Test often to avoid overcooking. Remove from oven the instant it is done, and refrigerate.

It is easy to make this into chocolate custard. Make 4 cups of cocoa and use this instead of milk, cutting down a bit on the sugar in the list of ingredients because of the sweetness in the cocoa.

DRIED APPLE PUDDING

1 cup dried apples	3 tablespoons butter
1 cup dark molasses	1 egg, well beaten
1 teaspoon cinnamon	1¼ cups flour
½ teaspoon ground cloves	1 teaspoon baking soda

Soak apples overnight in enough water to cover. Then cut softened apples into bite-size bits. With whatever moisture is left in pan, mix cut-up apples, molasses and spices. Put over medium heat and bring to a boil. Add butter and beat thoroughly. Then stir in the beaten egg.

Next add flour which has been mixed with baking soda and pour mixture into buttered baking dish. Bake at 325° for 45 minutes. Serve with your favorite pudding sauce.

CHOCOLATE DREAM

1 cup sugar	1½ teaspoons vanilla flavoring
½ cup milk	5 egg whites
2 squares baking chocolate	¼ teaspoon cream of tartar
¼ teaspoon salt	

Cook together sugar, milk and chocolate which has been cut into small bits or shaved into small sections for easy melting. When it has cooked enough so that a very soft ball is formed when a teaspoonful of syrup is dropped into cold water, remove from fire. Add vanilla and stir well.

Beat egg whites until foamy; add cream of tartar and salt, and beat until stiff. Slowly fold syrup into beaten egg whites. Pour into buttered baking dish. Set dish in pan of hot water and bake in slow oven (325°), until firm to the touch. This will take about 35 minutes. Serve with plenty of Custard Sauce (see page 186).

DEEP-DISH PEAR PIE

In Grandma's day almost every home had at least one pear tree in the yard. Few flowers can rival the beauty of pear blossoms and few perfumes can match the rare scents the warm spring breezes brought from the blossom-laden branches. Now pear trees are not so common, but here is a recipe from Grandma's old cookbook that can bring back memories of pleasant days long gone.

3 tablespoons lemon juice
½ teaspoon grated lemon rind
6 cups fresh pears, sliced
¾ cup dark brown sugar
2 tablespoons flour

½ teaspoon cinnamon
¼ teaspoon nutmeg
3 tablespoons butter
pastry for 1-crust pie (see page 165)

1 tablespoon white sugar

Sprinkle lemon juice and rind over pears. Sift together sugar, flour and spices and mix well with pears. Put mixture into well-buttered baking dish and dot top with butter. Place rolled-out pastry over top of dish as though making a pie. Fancy up the edges of pastry and cut gashes in center of pastry. Sprinkle with sugar and bake at 425° for 25 minutes so pears will be very tender. Serve warm or cold. A wedge of sage cheese goes with a serving of this pie as naturally as youth and love.

ORANGE INDIAN PUDDING

4 tablespoons corn meal	3 pints milk
1 cup molasses	½ cup dried orange peel
1 teaspoon salt	1½ cups cold milk

Put corn meal in bowl and mix in molasses and salt. Boil 3 pints milk, then pour it scalding hot over corn meal. Stir carefully until it is well blended and no lumps are present. Butter deep pudding dish, cover bottom with fragments of dried orange peel, and pour in meal and milk mixture. Last of all, gently pour cold milk over top. Bake for 4½ hours in hot oven (475°). Serve with rich cream or top milk.

Tastes differ so, the half cup of dried orange peel can be reduced or added to, according to the preferences of a particular family. If it covers the bottom of the baking dish it will suit most persons.

RHODE ISLAND HUCKLEBERRY PUDDING

This is a very old recipe and has no set quantities of ingredients. The procedure itself will be easy to follow.

Line deep pudding dish with slices of buttered white bread. Fill this with alternate layers of huckleberries and granulated sugar. Squeeze juice of 1 lemon over all. Cover top with slices of bread, buttered on both sides. Place old plate or thick lid on dish and bake at 300° for 1½ hours with dish in pan of hot water.

Take pudding from oven, spread over it meringue of white of egg beaten lightly with sugar in proportion of 1 tablespoon sugar to 1 egg, and return to oven long enough to turn meringue a light golden brown. The old recipes called for a hard sauce but Grandma's Pudding Sauce (see page 167) is recommended because of its liquid quality.

CAPE COD HUCKLEBERRY SLUMP

1 quart huckleberries
1 cup sugar

½ cup boiling water
dough for buttermilk
biscuits (see page 161)

Wash berries carefully and mix with sugar and boiling water. Put in large skillet or frying pan with deep sides, and simmer until berries are soft and there is an abundance of juice. Roll out dough as if for buttermilk biscuits but roll down to ⅛ inch in thickness. Cut into small squares the size of large postage stamps and drop into cooking berries. Cover and cook for 20 minutes. Turn berries, huckleberry syrup and dumplings out into serving dish or glass bowl and serve hot with plain or whipped cream.

SOUTH COUNTY APPLE DUMPLINGS

2 cups sugar
2 cups water
¼ teaspoon cinnamon
¼ teaspoon ground nutmeg
¼ cup butter

6 apples
2 cups flour
1 teaspoon salt
2 teaspoons baking powder
¾ cup shortening

½ cup milk

First make sauce in which to cook dumplings by combining sugar, water, cinnamon and nutmeg. Cook for 5 minutes, then add butter and push to back of stove. Next pare and core apples, which should be firm and tasty. Then sift flour, salt and baking powder together and work in shortening. Add milk and stir until flour is well moistened but no longer. Roll out on floured rolling board to ¼ inch thickness and cut into 6 5-inch squares. Place 1 apple on each square, sprinkle well with additional sugar and spices, and dot with butter. Pick up corners like a handkerchief to be made into a bag, and pinch together on top of apple. Place in greased baking tin with at least 1 inch between each dumpling. Pour warm sauce over apples and bake in moderate oven (375°) for ½ hour.

These dumplings, named for the southern county of Rhode Island, which the natives refuse to call Washington County, should be served hot with cream.

SQUASH PIE

1½ cups milk	1 teaspoon salt
2 eggs	¾ teaspoon ginger
2½ cups cooked or canned	¾ teaspoon nutmeg
squash, well mashed	1 unbaked 9-inch pastry shell
¾ cup sugar	(see page 165)
½ teaspoon cinnamon	

Heat milk and then beat eggs, adding milk slowly. Stir in squash and dry ingredients, making sure all is mixed well. Oven should be hot (450°), and unbaked pastry shell in pie tin, before mixture is prepared. Pour squash custard into pastry shell and place tin in oven. After 15 minutes in hot oven, reduce heat to 350° and continue baking for ½ hour. The filling will bake first near the edges, but care must be taken to see that center is also well cooked. Test often near end of baking period by inserting a silver knife blade. The blade should emerge clean, or the custard will not be done.

APPLE PAN DOWDY

3 cups sliced apples	⅓ cup granulated sugar
¼ teaspoon nutmeg	1 egg
⅓ teaspoon cinnamon	¾ cup flour
⅓ cup brown sugar, tamped down	¾ teaspoon baking powder
	¼ teaspoon salt
¼ cup butter	⅓ cup milk

Butter deep baking dish and place sliced apples in bottom. Sprinkle apples with spices and brown sugar. Bake in moderate oven (375°) for ½ hour. Cream butter and add sugar, a little at a time, and beat until light. Add egg and again beat well. Next add dry ingredients and milk, alternately, and beat until smooth. Pour mixture over apples, spreading it out to edges. Put dish back in oven and bake for another ½ hour.

Old-time Yankees served this dish with rich cream, but it can be served also with a foamy sauce or one like Grandma's Pudding Sauce (see page 167).

PUMPKIN CUSTARD

2 cups milk	⅔ cup maple syrup
5 eggs, well beaten	¼ teaspoon salt
1¼ cups cooked, strained pumpkin	¼ teaspoon nutmeg
¼ teaspoon cinnamon	

Bring milk *almost* to a boil. In large mixing bowl place eggs, pumpkin, syrup, salt, nutmeg and cinnamon. Beat with wooden spoon until smooth and well blended. Stir hot milk into pumpkin mixture. Pour into 1 large or 6 small baking dishes which have been well buttered. Set in pan of hot water. Bake 1 full hour at 350°. Test to see whether the custard is done by inserting a silver knife blade into the center. It should come out clean.

BAKED INDIAN PUDDING

4 cups rich milk	½ teaspoon salt
⅓ cup white corn meal	½ teaspoon cinnamon
½ cup molasses	¼ teaspoon ginger
¼ cup granulated sugar	¼ teaspoon nutmeg

Take 2½ cups milk and bring slowly to scalding point. Blend corn meal in ½ cup cold milk and slowly pour mixture into scalded milk. Cook for 20 minutes, stirring once in a while. Then add molasses, sugar, salt and spices. Pour mixture into buttered baking dish and bake in slow oven (325°) for 50 minutes. Then stir in remaining cup of cold milk. Return to oven and bake for 1½ hours. Indian Pudding should be served warm with cold, rich cream.

APPLE BROWN BETTY

4 cups bread crumbs	¾ cup brown sugar
½ cup melted butter	4 cups chopped apples
¾ teaspoon cinnamon	¼ cup butter
pinch of salt	1½ cups powdered sugar

2 tablespoons fresh lemon juice

Butter deep baking dish. Mix bread crumbs, which are best if about the size of lima beans, with melted butter, cinnamon, salt and sugar. Then place apples and bread crumbs in alternate layers until all are used. Bake in moderate oven (375°) for 1 hour. The top should be a rich autumn brown.

The hard sauce is made by creaming butter until soft and adding sugar. Then whip until very light and airy. Add lemon juice and stir it in.

YANKEE APPLE JOHN

6 large tart apples	2 cups flour
¾ cup sugar	½ teaspoon salt
1 teaspoon cinnamon	3 teaspoons baking powder
¾ teaspoon nutmeg	½ cup butter
2 tablespoons butter	⅔ cup milk

If apples are not large, use 7 or 8 smaller ones. Slice them thin after peeling and coring and place in bottom of baking dish. Mix sugar, cinnamon and nutmeg and sprinkle over apples. Dot with butter.

Next make biscuit dough by sifting flour, salt and baking powder together. Work in butter and add milk. Mix sufficiently to blend but no more. Knead dough lightly on floured board and roll out to cover baking dish. Place dough over apples and brush with milk to give pretty appearance when cooked. Bake in hot oven (425°) for 25 minutes and then reduce heat to 350° and cook until apples are done, about 20 minutes.

This old apple dessert was usually served with a nutmeg sauce, although it tastes excellent with a hard sauce or Grandma's Pudding Sauce (see page 167).

NUTMEG SAUCE

1 cup sugar   ⅛ teaspoon salt
¼ teaspoon nutmeg   2 cups boiling water
3 tablespoons flour   1 tablespoon cider vinegar

1 tablespoon butter

Mix well sugar, nutmeg, flour and salt, and stir in boiling water.
Cook over fire until thickened, being sure to stir constantly so
mixture comes out smooth and satiny. Remove from stove and
add vinegar and butter, blending them thoroughly.

APPLE SNOW

2 large tart apples   1¼ cups very fine sugar
¼ teaspoon salt   4 egg whites, beaten stiff

Peel and grate apples. Add salt and sugar. Beat egg whites very
stiff. Then very gently, but thoroughly, fold in grated apple
mixture. Chill and serve very cold with Boiled Custard as the
sauce (see page 177).

CUSTARD SAUCE

3 egg yolks   ⅛ teaspoon salt
1 cup milk   1 teaspoon vanilla flavoring
¾ cup sugar   1 teaspoon lemon juice

Beat egg yolks in small pan over low heat or in top of small
double boiler over gently boiling water. Stir in milk, sugar
and salt. Cook, stirring constantly, until mixture coats the
spoon. Then pour into serving bowl and add flavorings. Chill
before using.

FRENCH APPLE PIE

6 large tart apples	1 unbaked pastry shell (see
¾ cup sugar	page 165)
1 teaspoon cinnamon	1 cup sifted flour
½ teaspoon nutmeg	½ cup butter
2 teaspoons flour	½ cup dark brown sugar

Peel and slice apples, then mix in sugar, cinnamon, nutmeg and 2 teaspoons flour. Place in pastry shell, spreading evenly. Next cream butter and brown sugar; then add 1 cup flour to make a crumbly mixture. Spread over apples. Bake at 425° for 10 minutes. Reduce heat to 375° and bake for 45 minutes longer.

RHUBARB TAPIOCA

Grandma had to use pearl tapioca. Anyone wishing to use granulated tapioca should substitute ⅜ cup of that for the old-fashioned type. In this case no soaking in cold water is necessary. Just add boiling water to tapioca and proceed as below.

¾ cup pearl tapioca	3 cups rhubarb, cut in pieces
cold water to cover	1 cup sugar
2½ cups boiling water	⅛ teaspoon nutmeg
½ teaspoon salt	

Cover tapioca generously with cold water and allow to stand 1 hour at least, or overnight. Keep covered while soaking. If any water is not absorbed, use that much less boiling water. Add boiling water and salt to soaked tapioca and cook over direct heat until it comes to a boil. Then cook over boiling water in double boiler until tapioca is transparent. Place rhubarb in buttered baking dish, cover with sugar, sprinkle with nutmeg and pour tapioca over this. Bake about 20 minutes in moderate oven (350°) until rhubarb is soft. Serve hot or cold with Lemon Sauce or cream.

LEMON SAUCE

1 cup sugar
2 tablespoons flour

2 cups boiling water
1 lemon, juice and grated rind

2 tablespoons butter

Mix sugar and flour thoroughly. Slowly add boiling water. Cook 15 minutes over slow heat or in double boiler. Add juice, grated rind and butter. Stir again and serve.

OLD-TIME SUET PUDDING

½ cup suet, cut very fine
½ cup molasses
1 egg, beaten
½ cup milk or water
1½ cups sifted flour

½ teaspoon salt
¾ teaspoon baking soda
1 teaspoon cinnamon
½ teaspoon nutmeg
2 teaspoons baking powder

1 cup raisins

Mix together suet, molasses, egg and milk. Beat well. Sift dry ingredients together; mix with raisins and add to first mixture. Pour into well-greased mold. Steam for 2 hours. Serve hot with Grandma's Pudding Sauce (see page 167).

RHUBARB SHORTCAKE

2 cups flour, sifted
4 teaspoons baking powder
4 tablespoons sugar
½ teaspoon salt
2 tablespoons shortening

¼ cup cream
¾ cup milk
1 egg, well beaten
4 cups rhubarb, cut up
1 cup sugar

1 tablespoon lemon juice

Sift and mix dry ingredients together. Cut in shortening with fork or fingers. Add cream, milk and egg to make soft dough and mix thoroughly. Pour into greased cake pan and bake for 15 to 20 minutes at 425°. Turn out of pan and split. Just before serving, place layer of cooked rhubarb between layers of cake and pile it generously on top. To prepare cooked rhubarb mix sugar, lemon juice and rhubarb together and cook very slowly over low heat or in double boiler until rhubarb is tender but not mushy. When preparing rhubarb be sure to cut tops off but do not peel stalks.

RHUBARB DELIGHT

2¼ cups fine dry bread crumbs	½ teaspoon cinnamon
1½ cups light brown sugar	½ cup melted butter
2 tablespoons white sugar	6 cups rhubarb, cut up
¼ teaspoon salt	2 tablespoons lemon juice
¼ teaspoon nutmeg	1 tablespoon grated lemon rind

Mix together bread crumbs, sugars, salt and spices. Blend in butter. Mix rhubarb with lemon juice and rind. Into buttered pudding dish put alternate layers of rhubarb and crumb mixtures. Press crumb layers down well. Bake at 350° for 35 minutes, or until rhubarb is tender. This dish is excellent hot or cold. Serve with Custard Sauce (see page 186).

VERMONT MOUNTAIN PUDDING

½ cup maple syrup	3 tablespoons cornstarch
1½ cups milk	¼ cup cold milk
⅛ teaspoon salt	1½ teaspoons vanilla flavoring

Heat syrup, 1½ cups milk and salt together. Blend cornstarch into ¼ cup cold milk. Add slowly to hot mixture. Cook over hot water steadily until thickened. Cook an additional 5 minutes to kill off starchy taste, stirring all the while. Remove from heat. Add vanilla. Pour into dish or mold rinsed with cold water. Chill thoroughly. Turn out on serving dish and serve with plenty of rich cream.

STEAMED HUCKLEBERRY PUDDING

1½ cups sifted flour   1 teaspoon cinnamon
⅛ teaspoon salt   ½ teaspoon baking soda
½ teaspoon nutmeg   1 cup molasses
            2 cups cleaned fresh huckleberries

Sift flour, salt and spices together. Stir soda into molasses and add gradually to flour mixture. Beat well. Then fold in huckleberries, trying not to break too many berries. Pour into well-greased mold and steam for 2 hours. Serve hot with Lemon Sauce (see page 188).

This was a very economical dish, especially since Grandma used an old-fashioned stove, but its economy doesn't detract from its rare goodness.

OLD-FASHIONED BREAD PUDDING

4 slices buttered homemade   ¼ teaspoon salt
   bread, cut up   ½ teaspoon nutmeg
½ cup raisins   1 teaspoon cinnamon
3 eggs, slightly beaten   ½ teaspoon vanilla flavoring
¼ cup sugar   ½ teaspoon lemon flavoring
            2½ cups milk

Have at hand a buttered baking dish. Place bread pieces in it. Mix raisins lightly with bread. Mix together eggs, sugar, spices, flavorings and milk. Pour over bread. Bake at 325° for 45 minutes. Serve with Grandma's Pudding Sauce (see page 167).

BOSTON CREAM PIE

1 cup sifted flour	½ teaspoon vanilla flavoring
1½ teaspoons baking powder	1½ teaspoons lemon juice
¼ teaspoon salt	1 cup sugar, sifted
4 egg yolks	4 egg whites, beaten stiff
⅓ cup milk	but not dry

Sift together flour, baking powder and salt. Beat together egg yolks, milk and flavorings. Add sugar and beat until smooth and light. Gradually blend in dry ingredients, stirring thoroughly. Gently fold in egg whites. Pour into 2 greased and floured layer pans. Bake at 325° for 35 minutes. Cool on cake racks.

BOSTON CREAM PIE FILLING

1 cup hot milk	⅛ teaspoon salt
2 tablespoons butter	½ cup cold milk
⅓ cup flour	2 egg yolks, slightly beaten
⅓ cup sugar	1 teaspoon vanilla flavoring
1 teaspoon lemon juice	

Put milk and butter in top of double boiler. Bring *almost* to a boil over boiling water. Mix flour, sugar and salt together. Blend to a smooth sauce with cold milk. Then very slowly add, stirring, to hot milk mixture. Cook until thick. Blend a little of this mixture into beaten egg yolk and add latter to thickened milk mixture on stove. Blend smoothly and cook about 2 more minutes. Add flavoring and cool. Spread filling between layers of cake to make the pie, and dust top layer with powdered sugar.

CHERRY SAUCE

Grandma made this often to pour over plain cake, or to use up dry cake such as sponge, angel food or butter varieties.

1 cup white sugar	3 cups cherry juice
1½ tablespoons cornstarch	1 cup water
¼ teaspoon salt	2 tablespoons butter
2 tablespoons lemon juice	

Mix thoroughly all dry ingredients. Bring cherry juice and water to a boil. Slowly blend a little hot juice into dry ingredients. Then stir mixture slowly into boiling juice. Cook, stirring constantly, until thickened and smooth like very heavy cream. Add butter and beat well. Stir in lemon juice.

HUCKLEBERRY POT-PIE

1 cup sugar	4 cups fresh huckleberries
½ teaspoon cinnamon	2 tablespoons lemon juice
¼ teaspoon nutmeg	2 tablespoons butter
3½ tablespoons flour	unbaked pastry top (see
2 tablespoons maple sugar	page 165)
¼ teaspoon salt	1 teaspoon milk

Butter a baking dish. Mix dry ingredients together. Blend lightly with berries. Put into baking dish. Pour lemon juice over all and dot with butter. Cover top of dish with a rolled plain pastry. Make a fancy fluted rim. Cut gashes into top with sharp knife and brush with milk. Bake at 400° for 40 minutes. Serve with cream.

CHERRY PUDDING IN-A-HURRY

½ cup sugar
1 cup sifted flour
1 teaspoon baking powder
¼ teaspoon cinnamon
¼ teaspoon salt

¼ cup melted butter
½ cup milk
1 teaspoon vanilla flavoring
2 cups fresh pitted cherries
½ cup sugar

1 cup hot cherry juice

Mix together ½ cup sugar, flour, baking powder, cinnamon and salt. Add melted butter, milk and flavoring. Beat hard. Have ready a buttered baking pan. Pour batter into it and cover with cherries mixed with ½ cup sugar. Pour hot cherry juice over this. Bake at 350° for 40 minutes. Serve hot with cream or milk.

This was a quick and easy dessert Grandma used to fix, usually when pitting and canning the cherries. After all, even though busy, she had to eat, and these ingredients were very handy.

APPLES BAKED IN HONEY

6 medium-sized apples, peeled,
   cored and quartered
1 tablespoon water

⅓ cup honey
2 tablespoons butter
1 teaspoon cinnamon

1 teaspoon sugar

Place apple quarters in buttered baking dish. Pour over them water and honey. Dot with butter. Mix cinnamon and sugar and sprinkle over all. Bake at 350° until apples are tender, about 30 minutes. This dish can be eaten with good results hot or cold, with or without cream or milk.

RHUBARB AND STRAWBERRY TREAT

3 cups fresh rhubarb, cut up but   ¾ cup water
   not peeled   1 cup strawberries, washed
¾ cup sugar   and hulled

Cook rhubarb with sugar and water until almost tender. Add whole strawberries and cook gently for 4 minutes. Chill well before serving.

RHUBARB PIE

3 cups rhubarb, cut up   pastry for 2-crust pie (see
1¼ cups sugar   page 166)
3 tablespoons flour   2 tablespoons butter
⅛ teaspoon salt   ¼ teaspoon nutmeg
            1 teaspoon milk

Prepare rhubarb by picking tender, young stalks and cutting off leaves and bottoms. Wash thoroughly, but do not peel. Cut into pieces about 1½ inches in length.

Mix together rhubarb, sugar, flour and salt. Fill pastry-lined pie pan. Dot with butter and sprinkle on nutmeg. Adjust top crust. Flute edges and prick top of crust. Brush with milk. Bake in hot oven (425°) for 10 minutes. Then finish at 350° for 30 minutes.

AUNT PATIENCE'S MAPLE BUTTERNUT PIE

2 cups milk   1½ teaspoons vanilla flavoring
1 cup maple sugar   ¼ teaspoon salt
3 tablespoons cornstarch   1 baked pastry shell (see
¼ cup cold milk   page 165)
3 egg yolks, beaten   ¾ cup butternuts, chopped fine
1 tablespoon butter   3 tablespoons sifted sugar
       3 egg whites, beaten stiff

Put milk and maple sugar in top of double boiler over boiling water and heat until sugar is dissolved. Mix cornstarch with cold milk. Blend mixture slowly into hot milk, stirring until it thickens. Remove part of this and blend into beaten egg yolks. Then return to mixture, beating until smooth and well blended. Cook 3 minutes more, stirring constantly. Remove from heat. Add butter, vanilla and salt. Cool. Pour into baked pastry shell. Sprinkle chopped butternuts over surface. Cover with meringue made by blending 3 tablespoons sugar into stiffly beaten egg whites. Brown meringue lightly in moderate oven (350°).

DRIED PEACH PIE

2½ cups cooked dried peaches	2 tablespoons cornstarch
1 cup peach juice, unsweetened	2 tablespoons cold water
1 cup sugar	2½ tablespoons butter
¼ teaspoon nutmeg	1 teaspoon lemon flavoring
½ teaspoon salt	pastry for 2-crust pie (see page 166)

1 teaspoon milk

Combine peaches, juice, sugar, nutmeg and salt. Bring to a boil. Mix cornstarch with water. Blend into hot peach mixture, stirring constantly. Cook 3 minutes, stirring all the time. Add butter and flavoring. Cool to room temperature. Pour into pastry-lined pie pan. Cover with other pastry shell, and slash with sharp knife. Flute the edges. Brush top with milk and bake in hot oven (450°) for 10 minutes. Reduce heat to 375° and bake for 20 more minutes, or until nicely browned.

HOMEMADE STRAWBERRY ICE CREAM*

2 quarts fresh strawberries | 2 tablespoons lemon juice
1 cup white sugar | 1 quart cream
2 quarts Boiled Custard (see page 177)

Wash, hull and chop strawberries. Mix lightly with sugar. Cover and let stand at room temperature for at least 1 hour. Add lemon juice. Mix cream and custard together until smooth. Then add strawberry mixture.

Pour into freezer, being sure it is no more than ¾ full. Insert dasher, tighten cover and place in ice bucket. Use 8 parts chopped ice to 1 part coarse salt. Turn freezer slowly until cream is frozen. Remove dasher, fasten cover again, plugging hole so salt water does not gain entry, and repack in ice bucket. This time use 4 parts ice to 1 part salt. Cover well and allow to stand *at least* 1 hour before serving.

LEMON MERINGUE PIE

1½ cups white sugar | 3 tablespoons butter
7 tablespoons cornstarch | 4 tablespoons strained lemon
1½ cups boiling water | juice
3 large egg yolks, beaten well | 1 baked pastry shell (see page 165)

In top of double boiler mix sugar and cornstarch evenly together. Slowly add boiling water, stirring well to avoid formation of lumps. Place over boiling water; stir constantly until

---

* For making this ice cream in a modern electric refrigerator one needs only to use the same mixture as given above and do the freezing in the ice-cube compartment. Since all refrigerators are not alike, it is advisable that the instruction book that comes with each model be followed closely.

mixture thickens well. Continue cooking at least 5 minutes, still stirring all the time. Remove a little of this mixture and blend into egg yolks. Stir this slowly into hot mixture in top of double boiler. Cook for 5 minutes more. Remove from heat; add butter and juice, blending well. Cool. Pour into baked pastry shell. Cover with meringue, making sure meringue touches sides of pan all around. Bake at 325° for 15 minutes, or until browned as desired.

MERINGUE

3 large egg whites   3 tablespoons sugar
¼ teaspoon cream of tartar

Beat whites lightly. Add cream of tartar. Beat until it forms peaks. Fold in sugar, beating until shiny.

DOUGHNUTS

½ cup sugar   2¼ cups flour
1 tablespoon melted butter   2½ teaspoons baking powder
2 eggs, well beaten   ¼ teaspoon salt
1 teaspoon vanilla flavoring   ½ teaspoon nutmeg
½ cup milk   fat for frying
powdered sugar

Add white sugar and melted butter to eggs, and beat thoroughly. Add vanilla and milk, beating well. Sift dry ingredients together. Add to egg mixture. Beat thoroughly again. This should give a soft dough. Put out on lightly floured board and roll until a little less than ½ inch thick. Cut with doughnut cutter. Fry in deep fat. A thermometer for deep fat frying should register 380°. If no thermometer is available, fat is ready if it browns a small piece of white bread in 1 minute. Fat *must* be hot enough so that doughnuts will not absorb it. When doughnuts come to surface of fat and are brown on one side turn them over with long-handled fork and brown other side. Remove to drain. Sprinkle powdered sugar just before serving.

Grandma always fried the "holes" and gave them to any children who might be around. They were considered a rare treat.

MASHED POTATO DOUGHNUTS

2 eggs, well beaten	1 teaspoon salt
1 cup sugar	½ teaspoon nutmeg
1 cup mashed potatoes	½ teaspoon baking soda
4 cups sifted flour	1 cup buttermilk
3 teaspoons baking powder	4 tablespoons melted butter

fat for frying

Beat together beaten eggs and melted butter. Add sugar and cream mixture thoroughly. Then add mashed potatoes, buttermilk and flour which has been sifted together with baking powder, soda, salt and nutmeg to make it light; blending all together very well. This should produce a dough which is light and easy to handle. Put it out on lightly floured board and roll to ½ inch thickness. Cut with doughnut cutter. Drop doughnuts into deep fat which has reached 360°. Fry only five or six at a time. As the doughnuts rise to the surface turn them with a long fork so they become brown on both sides. It requires about 3 minutes for the doughnuts to cook through and turn a golden brown. As each one is sufficiently browned remove it from the fat and drain in a wire basket or on parchment paper. Sugar doughnuts if desired.

BLACK CAPS IN A BLANKET

2 cups sifted flour
4 tablespoons sugar
¼ teaspoon salt
1 cup shortening
  cold water to dampen dough

1 cup black raspberry jam
2 teaspoons lemon juice
2 tablespoons butter
1 teaspoon milk
  dash of cinnamon

Sift flour, sugar and salt together. Mix in shortening with fork or fingers. Work it in lightly. Add as little water as possible; just enough to hold dough together. Roll out into oblong shape on floured board until about ¼ inch thick. Mix jam and lemon juice together and spread on dough. Dot with butter. Roll dough up as if for a jelly roll, and press open ends together so juices will not escape. Put into greased and floured pan and brush top with milk. Sprinkle a dash of cinnamon over top if desired. Bake at 375° for 20 minutes, or until well done and nicely browned. Serve with Grandma's hot Pudding Sauce (see page 167) or with cold Custard Sauce (see page 186).

OLD CONNECTICUT PEACH PUDDING

1 teaspoon vanilla flavoring
3 tablespoons butter
  grated rind of 1 lemon
¼ cup sugar
2 egg yolks
1 cup flour
¼ teaspoon salt

3 teaspoons baking powder
½ cup milk
10 large ripe peaches
1½ tablespoons lemon juice
¾ cup sugar
2 tablespoons sugar
2 egg whites, beaten stiff

¼ teaspoon cinnamon

Blend together vanilla, butter, grated lemon rind, ¼ cup sugar and egg yolks. Beat thoroughly. Sift together flour, salt and baking powder and add alternately with milk to first mixture, beating well. Butter baking dish and fill bottom with peaches which have been peeled, stoned and quartered. Sprinkle with lemon juice. Then lightly mix in ¾ cup sugar. Pour pudding mixture over peaches and bake at 350° for 25 minutes. Remove from oven and cover with meringue made by slowly adding 2 tablespoons sugar to egg whites and beating until stiff. Dust with cinnamon and return dish to oven to brown meringue. This will take 15 minutes, or longer if you prefer darker topping. Serve warm as it is, or with cream or Grandma's Pudding Sauce (see page 167).

APPLE POCKET-BOOKS

¾ cup dark brown sugar
½ teaspoon cinnamon
3 tablespoons flour
¼ teaspoon salt
½ cup water
2 tablespoons butter

1 teaspoon lemon juice
4 large apples, peeled and
chopped
2 cups sifted flour
½ teaspoon salt
⅔ cup shortening

4 tablespoons milk

In saucepan mix brown sugar, cinnamon, flour and salt thoroughly. Slowly add water. Then cook over low heat, stirring, until thickened. Add butter and lemon juice. Remove from heat and add apples. Cool.

Next mix 2 cups flour, salt and shortening together as for pie crust. Add milk, and mix with fork or fingers. Lift out onto floured board and roll to ¼ inch thickness. Cut into squares (3- to 5-inch squares are best), and on each square put 1 spoonful of apple mixture. Fold over to form a triangle, seal edges

and prick tops. Put on greased baking sheet and bake at 425°
for 15 minutes.

Delicious hot with Grandma's Pudding Sauce (see page 167),
and very good cold too.

BANBURY TARTS

The filling:

2 teaspoons flour	½ cup raisins, chopped fine
1 cup sugar	4½ tablespoons orange juice
5 figs, chopped fine	1½ tablespoons lemon juice
½ cup currants, chopped fine	1 tablespoon water

½ cup butternuts, chopped

Mix flour and sugar together. Then mix this with all other ingredients except nuts in top of double boiler. Put over boiling
water and cook 30 minutes. Remove from fire and stir in
chopped nuts. Cool.

The pastry:

3 cups flour	¾ teaspoon salt
¼ teaspoon baking powder	¾ cup shortening

ice water to dampen dough

Sift flour, baking powder and salt into mixing bowl. Add shortening and blend all with fork. Add ice water by the tablespoonful, mixing gently until dough comes away from sides of bowl.
Put out on floured board and roll out to about ¼ inch thickness
and cut into 3-inch squares. Put 2 teaspoons filling on each
square, fold over each filled square to form a triangle. Press
edges of dough together with fork. Make small slits in tops with
knife and brush tops with milk. Bake at 450° for 20 minutes.

FRIED APPLE PIES

3 cups flour

1 teaspoon baking powder

½ teaspoon salt

6 tablespoons butter

¾ cup milk

1½ cups sweetened applesauce

2 teaspoons cinnamon

fat for frying

powdered sugar

Sift flour, baking powder and salt into large bowl. Cut in butter with fork. Add milk and stir all well. Put on floured board and roll thin. Cut in 2-inch squares. Place 2 teaspoonfuls applesauce on each square and sprinkle with cinnamon. Fold over to form triangles and seal edges tightly with fork. Do *not* make any openings in crust as you do for other pies. Fry in deep fat (375°) until pies have desired brownness. Drain on absorbent paper. Dust with sugar. This dessert is good served hot with maple syrup or cream, and just as good cold.

Chapter 27

Cakes and Cookies

BLACKBERRY JAM CAKE

½ cup butter
1 cup dark brown sugar,
   packed down
3 eggs, separated
1¾ cups flour
1 teaspoon baking soda

½ teaspoon ground cloves
1 teaspoon nutmeg
1 teaspoon cinnamon
¼ teaspoon allspice
3 tablespoons sour milk
1 cup blackberry jam

¾ cup raisins, chopped

Cream together butter and sugar until light. Add beaten egg yolks. Sift dry ingredients together. Blend sour milk and jam.

Add dry mixture alternately with jam mixture into butter and sugar mixture. Beat well. Stir in raisins, well floured. Gently fold into this beaten egg whites. Bake in 2 layers at 375° for 25 minutes.

Almost any frosting may be used. Grandma used this one:

CINNAMON FROSTING

2 cups confectioner's sugar	2 tablespoons light cream
½ teaspoon cinnamon	1 teaspoon lemon flavoring
2 tablespoons butter	1 teaspoon vanilla flavoring

pinch of salt

Mix ingredients together and beat until smooth and fluffy before spreading on both layers of jam cake.

CRANBERRY SPICE CAKE

½ cup butter	½ teaspoon cloves
1½ cups sifted sugar	½ teaspoon nutmeg
3 egg yolks, beaten	¼ cup sour milk
2 cups sifted flour	1½ cups cranberry jelly
1 teaspoon baking powder	3 egg whites, beaten stiff
1 teaspoon baking soda	fruit juice
1 teaspoon cinnamon	confectioner's sugar
½ teaspoon allspice	2 tablespoons melted butter

Cream butter and sugar and add egg yolks. Beat until light and fluffy. Sift dry ingredients together. Beat in sour milk alternately with mixed dry ingredients. Whip in jelly and fold in egg whites. Pour into greased and floured loaf pan. Bake for 1 hour in moderate oven (350°).

When cake is cool, frost with a little fruit juice mixed with enough confectioner's sugar to stiffen, and add melted butter. Beat frosting smooth before spreading.

YANKEE FRUIT CAKE

This is an old recipe in the Larkin and Stedman families. It entails a little more work than most cakes but is well worth the effort. Grandma frosted it sometimes, and sometimes she just dusted it with confectioner's sugar. Never use a butter frosting if you intend to keep the cake a long time and let it "ripen."

1 cup fat salt pork
2 cups raw apples, cut up
1 cup brown sugar
1 cup molasses
4 tablespoons citron, chopped fine
1 cup seedless raisins
½ cup preserved peels
1 cup seeded muscat raisins
1 cup flour
3 eggs, beaten
2 cups flour

2 teaspoons baking soda
2 teaspoons cream of tartar
1 teaspoon allspice
½ teaspoon ground cloves
½ teaspoon nutmeg
½ teaspoon mace
2 teaspoons cinnamon
1 cup chopped butternuts
½ teaspoon salt
1 cup candied cherries, if
    desired for decorating

Run salt pork through food chopper. Put into saucepan ground pork, apples cut into small pieces, brown sugar and molasses. Simmer slowly for 30 minutes. Add citron, seedless raisins and peels. Mix well over heat; then cool.

Mix seeded raisins with 1 cup flour, then cut in pieces. Add seeded raisins to original cooled mixture in large mixing bowl. Add beaten eggs.

Sift remaining dry ingredients together. Add fruit and egg mixture, beating in thoroughly, and follow with chopped nuts and salt. When well mixed, put in greased and floured square pan. If cherries are used, press onto top of cake. Bake in slow oven (325°) for 1 hour.

Do not frost until cool.

MISSIONARY CAKE

½ cup butter	½ teaspoon cloves
1½ cups sifted sugar	½ teaspoon nutmeg
2 egg yolks	1 cup buttermilk
2 cups sifted flour	2 ounces unsweetened chocolate
1½ teaspoons baking soda	1 cup chopped raisins
1 teaspoon cinnamon	½ cup chopped nuts

Cream sugar and butter together. Add egg yolks and beat until light and fluffy. Sift dry ingredients together. Add alternately with buttermilk to butter and egg mixture. Blend in chocolate, which has been melted over hot water, and add raisins and nuts. Bake in layers at 375° for 30 minutes.

MISSIONARY CAKE FROSTING

2 cups sugar	⅛ teaspoon cream of tartar
½ cup water	2 egg whites, well beaten
1 ounce unsweetened chocolate	1 teaspoon vanilla flavoring

Boil sugar, water, chocolate and cream of tartar till a teaspoonful of mixture makes a soft ball when dropped in cold water.

Pour *half* the syrup over egg whites, beating constantly. Cook remaining syrup 3 minutes longer. Then add to first mixture, beating constantly. Add vanilla. Then beat until stiff enough to spread.

DRIED APPLE CAKE

2 cups dried apples	1 teaspoon baking soda
1 cup molasses	1 teaspoon cloves
1½ cups brown sugar	1 teaspoon allspice
1 cup butter	1 teaspoon cinnamon
3 eggs, well beaten	½ teaspoon nutmeg
3½ cups sifted flour	½ cup sour milk

Soak dried apples overnight in just enough water to cover fruit. In the morning drain well and chop apples fine. Then add molasses. Let simmer slowly until tender. Cool. Mix brown sugar and butter and add eggs. Mix until light. Then stir in apple mixture. Sift dry ingredients together and add alternately with sour milk. Bake in layers or in a loaf in moderate oven (350°) for 30 minutes.

Sea-foam frosting makes an excellent topping for this moist cake.

SEA-FOAM FROSTING

½ cup dark brown sugar	¼ cup water
1 cup white sugar	2 tablespoons strong coffee
¼ teaspoon cream of tartar	2 egg whites
⅛ teaspoon salt	1 teaspoon vanilla flavoring

Boil together sugars, cream of tartar, salt, water and coffee, *without stirring,* until syrup spins a long thread from a spoon. Remove from fire at once. Beat egg whites very stiff. Slowly add syrup, beating constantly. Add vanilla. Continue to beat until mixture holds its shape and is of right consistency to spread. Use between layers and on tops and sides of cakes as desired.

AUNT ANNIE'S RAISED CAKE

2 cups bread dough
1 cup sugar
½ cup butter
½ teaspoon baking powder

1 teaspoon vanilla flavoring
1 teaspoon lemon flavoring
¼ teaspoon nutmeg
½ teaspoon cinnamon

½ cup seedless raisins

Mix ingredients together and beat thoroughly. Put into well-buttered tube pan. Let rise until double in bulk. Bake about 1 hour in slow oven (325°). Test during last part of baking to avoid overbaking. Frost, if desired, or dust with powdered sugar.

SQUASH CAKE

1 cup dark brown sugar
1 cup white sugar
½ cup butter
1 cup cooked yellow squash
2 eggs, well beaten

3 cups sifted flour
4 teaspoons baking powder
¼ teaspoon baking soda
½ cup milk
1 teaspoon vanilla flavoring

1 teaspoon lemon flavoring

Cream sugars and butter. Add squash, which should have been beaten smooth, and eggs to creamed mixture, and beat thoroughly. Sift together dry ingredients. Add alternately with milk to squash mixture, beating well after each addition. Beat in flavorings. Bake in large greased and floured tube pan, or 3 greased and floured layer pans. Bake at 350° for 30 minutes. Cool on cake racks. Sea-foam Frosting (see page 207) is recommended for this cake.

WINDHAM COUNTY APPLESAUCE CAKE

½ cup butter
½ teaspoon salt
1½ cups sugar
3 eggs, beaten
2 cups plus 2 tablespoons flour
1½ teaspoons baking soda
¾ teaspoon baking powder
1 teaspoon cinnamon

¼ teaspoon cloves
½ teaspoon nutmeg
¼ teaspoon mace
¼ teaspoon allspice
2½ tablespoons cocoa
1¾ cups unsweetened applesauce
¾ cup black walnut meats, if
   desired

1 cup chopped raisins

Cream together butter, salt and sugar. Add eggs and beat until light and fluffy. Sift together twice flour, soda, baking powder and spices to mix them well. Add dry ingredients alternately with applesauce to creamed mixture. Beat well after each addition until smooth. Mix in raisins. Add the chopped walnuts, if desired.

Pour into greased and floured pan. Bake in moderate oven (350°) for 60 minutes, or until done. A 10-inch square pan will give about the right thickness to the cake.

Grandma served this applesauce cake, both hot and cold, with big wedges of sage cheese. With a glass of milk, it was almost a meal in itself. Many's the time the cake, cheese and milk stayed a small boy's hunger between the close of school and supper at the end of the day.

GINGERSNAPS

1 cup shortening
2 cups dark brown sugar
1 egg, well beaten
1 cup molasses
4 cups flour

½ teaspoon salt
2 teaspoons baking soda
2 teaspoons ginger
1 teaspoon lemon flavoring
1 teaspoon vanilla flavoring

sugar for sprinkling tops

First cream shortening and brown sugar together very smoothly. Then blend in egg and molasses, beating until light and fluffy. With sifter mix flour, salt, soda and ginger together, and then mix them into previous batter. When dough is soft add liquid flavorings. Chill mixture for about 4 hours, or until easily handled with lightly floured hands. Shape into small balls and place on greased cookie tin. Do not press flat; they will fall and spread out when in oven. Bake in moderate oven (350°) for 14 minutes. Sprinkle with sugar and remove from tin with spatula.

PRUNE SPICE CAKE

1 cup sugar	1⅓ cups flour
½ cup butter	½ teaspoon baking soda
2 eggs, beaten	½ teaspoon baking powder
⅔ cup stewed prunes	½ teaspoon salt
⅔ cup buttermilk	½ teaspoon nutmeg
	1 teaspoon cinnamon

Blend together sugar, butter and eggs, beating until smooth and light. Add prunes, which have been pitted and chopped. Stir in buttermilk. Sift together dry ingredients and add to buttermilk mixture. Beat well. Pour into 2 greased and floured layer pans. Bake at 350° for 25 minutes. Cool. Use Prune Frosting.

PRUNE FROSTING

2 cups confectioner's sugar	1 tablespoon lemon juice
2 tablespoons butter	1 teaspoon cinnamon
2 tablespoons prune juice	¼ teaspoon salt

Mix 1 cup sugar with butter. Add remaining sugar and juices. Stir well. Add cinnamon and salt. Beat until creamy. Spread between layers and on top of cake when cake is cool.

AUNT ANNIE'S MOCHA CAKE

½ cup butter
1 cup sifted sugar
¼ teaspoon salt
1 teaspoon vanilla flavoring

2 eggs
2 cups flour
2 teaspoons baking powder
¾ cup milk

Cream together butter, sugar and salt. Add vanilla and eggs. Beat until creamy, light and fluffy. Sift flour and baking powder together. Add alternately with milk to creamed mixture, beating well after each addition. Beat until smooth and pour into 2 well-buttered and floured cake pans. Bake at 350° for 25 minutes. Cool on cake racks. Use Mocha Frosting.

MOCHA FROSTING

4 tablespoons butter
⅛ teaspoon salt
1 teaspoon vanilla flavoring
2½ tablespoons strong coffee

2½ to 3 cups confectioner's sugar, sifted
2 tablespoons cocoa

Cream butter, salt and vanilla. Mix 2 cups sugar and cocoa together. Add alternately with coffee to butter mixture. Beat thoroughly. Add more sifted sugar, beating each time, until right consistency for spreading.

MARBLE CAKE

½ cup butter
1¼ cups sugar
½ teaspoon salt
2 eggs, beaten
1½ teaspoons vanilla flavoring
2 cups flour
3 teaspoons baking powder

1 cup milk
2 squares unsweetened
    baking chocolate, melted
½ teaspoon nutmeg
1 teaspoon cinnamon
¼ teaspoon ground cloves
¼ teaspoon ground allspice

Cream together butter, sugar and salt. Add eggs and vanilla and beat thoroughly until creamy and light. Sift flour and baking powder together and add alternately with milk to creamed mixture. Divide batter into 2 parts. To one half of batter add melted chocolate and spices and beat thoroughly until well blended. Have ready greased and floured square cake pan (about 8 x 12 inches). Put batter in pan by alternating spoonfuls from light and dark batters. Bake at 350° for 40 minutes. Remove from pan and cool on racks. Frost as desired.

OLD-FASHIONED CITRON CAKE

1 cup light brown sugar
½ cup butter
2 large eggs, well beaten
1 teaspoon vanilla flavoring
1 teaspoon lemon flavoring
2 cups sifted flour

3 teaspoons baking powder
¼ teaspoon salt
½ teaspoon nutmeg
1 teaspoon cinnamon
¾ cup cold water
¾ cup citron, chopped fine

powdered sugar

Cream sugar and butter. Add eggs and flavorings and beat until light and fluffy. Sift dry ingredients together. Add alternately with water to creamed mixture. Beat well. Gently fold in chopped citron. Put into greased and floured loaf pan and bake at 350° for 1 hour. Sprinkle powdered sugar over cake while still warm.

SPONGE DROPS

⅓ cup sifted white sugar
2 egg whites, beaten stiff
2 egg yolks, beaten light

1 teaspoon lemon flavoring
1 teaspoon vanilla flavoring
⅓ cup sifted flour

⅛ teaspoon salt

Beat sugar gradually into stiffened egg whites. Gradually add egg yolks and flavorings. Fold in well-sifted flour and salt. Drop from spoon onto greased baking sheet. Bake at 325° until lightly browned.

According to Grandma, a cook needed "a light hand" for these cookies. The fluffiness of the batter is due mainly to the air that is whipped into the eggs.

SUGAR COOKIES

½ cup softened butter
¾ cup sugar
1 egg
1 tablespoon milk
1 teaspoon vanilla flavoring

1 teaspoon lemon flavoring
3 cups sifted flour (approx.)
1 teaspoon baking powder
¼ teaspoon nutmeg
sugar for sprinkling tops

Cream butter and sugar. Add egg, milk, and flavorings. Beat until very light. Add 1 cup flour with baking powder and nutmeg. Beat well. Then stir in enough of remaining flour to make dough stiff enough to roll. It may take all, and sometimes requires a bit more. Put dough out on lightly floured board. Roll very thin and cut into shapes with cookie cutters. Lift gently onto greased baking pans. Sprinkle with sugar. Bake at 425° until lightly browned, about 5 minutes. If you want to decorate the cookies in any way, do so *after* they have been placed on baking sheets. Cool before storing.

OLD-TIME RAISIN DROP COOKIES

2½ cups raisins
1 cup water
1 teaspoon baking soda
1 cup butter
2 cups sugar
3 eggs, beaten
1 teaspoon vanilla

1 teaspoon lemon
4 cups flour, sifted
1½ teaspoons baking powder
½ teaspoon salt
1 teaspoon cinnamon
¼ teaspoon nutmeg
¼ teaspoon allspice

1 cup chopped nuts, if desired

Wash and drain raisins and put them in saucepan. Add water. Boil for 5 minutes. Cool. Stir in soda. In the meantime cream butter and sugar. Add eggs and flavorings and beat until light and fluffy. Add cooled raisins. Sift together remaining dry ingredients and stir into first mixture, blending well. If nuts are used, add them now. Drop by teaspoon onto well-greased baking pan. Be sure to leave space between cookies as they will spread as they cook. Bake at 425° for 15 minutes, or until nicely browned top and bottom. Remove at once to cake racks to cool. Store, tightly covered, to keep them soft. Makes about 5 dozen.

AUTUMN SPICE CAKE

1 cup dark brown sugar	¼ teaspoon salt
½ cup melted butter	2¼ cups flour
1 large egg	3 teaspoons baking powder
2 egg yolks	1 teaspoon cinnamon
1 teaspoon vanilla flavoring	½ teaspoon nutmeg

1 cup milk

Mix together sugar, butter, eggs, flavoring and salt. Beat all until light and fluffy. Sift flour, baking powder and spices together. Add alternately with milk to sugar mixture, beating well after each addition. Pour into greased and floured square pan. Cover with meringue and bake at 350° for 45 minutes. The recipe for the meringue is:

2 egg whites	1 cup light brown sugar

½ teaspoon cinnamon

Beat egg whites stiff and add sugar and cinnamon.

HOT APPLE CAKE

1½ cups sliced apples	¼ teaspoon cloves
¾ cup molasses	¼ teaspoon nutmeg
2½ cups flour	¼ teaspoon allspice
½ cup sugar	1½ teaspoons baking soda
¼ teaspoon salt	⅓ cup melted butter
1 teaspoon cinnamon	½ cup water

1 egg, beaten very light

Cook apples slowly in molasses until tender, then cool. Sift all dry ingredients together. Add gradually to butter and water. Beat thoroughly. Stir in apples and molasses and mix well. Last of all add egg, stirring it in lightly. Bake in greased and floured shallow pan at 350° for 35 minutes. This is delicious served warm with a sauce like Grandma's Pudding Sauce (see page 167). It's good cold, too.

OLD FAITHFUL CAKE

This yellow cake was the standard cake in Grandma's home. It was eaten plain, frosted most often with chocolate icing, or served with berries and crushed fruit. Often it was the base for a simple dessert with Custard Sauce (see page 186) or Cherry Sauce on it (see page 192). Grandma could mix it in her sleep—and it always turned out wonderfully.

½ cup butter	1 teaspoon vanilla flavoring
1 cup sifted sugar	1 teaspoon lemon flavoring
3 eggs, well beaten	2 cups flour
¼ teaspoon salt	2½ teaspoons baking powder

⅔ cup milk

Cream butter and add sugar, then eggs, salt and flavorings. Beat until very light and fluffy. Sift flour and baking powder together. Add alternately with milk to creamed mixture, beating hard after each addition. Pour into 2 greased and floured layer pans. Bake at 350° for 35 minutes, or until done. Use cake tester to be sure. Remove to cake racks to cool.

CHOCOLATE FROSTING

1½ cups dark brown sugar	¼ cup butter
4 squares baking chocolate	¾ cup cold water
½ teaspoon salt	2 teaspoons vanilla flavoring
sifted confectioner's sugar	

Into heavy saucepan put brown sugar, chocolate which has been cut to bits, salt, butter and water. Mix thoroughly and bring to a boil. Cook 5 minutes, stirring constantly. Remove from stove and add vanilla, beating it in well. Add enough sifted confectioner's sugar to make frosting the right consistency to spread. Put between layers and over top of cooled cake.

HONEY FROSTING

1 egg white, unbeaten	2 tablespoons water
⅓ cup strained honey	⅛ teaspoon salt
3 tablespoons sugar	1 teaspoon lemon flavoring
½ teaspoon vanilla flavoring	

Put egg white, honey, sugar, water and salt in top of double boiler. Mix. Put over gently boiling water. Beat with rotary type egg beater constantly until frosting forms in peaks. This usually requires from 6 to 10 minutes. Add flavorings and frosting is ready to use.

SURPRISE COOKIES

Filling	*Cooky dough*
¾ pound seedless raisins	¼ cup butter, softened
1 cup shelled butternuts	⅓ cup sugar
1 large apple	1 egg, well beaten
1 tablespoon brown sugar	2 cups flour
1 tablespoon lemon juice	2 teaspoons baking powder
1 teaspoon cinnamon	¼ teaspoon salt
½ teaspoon nutmeg	½ cup confectioner's sugar
	1 tablespoon cream

Prepare filling first. Chop raisins, nuts and apple *very* fine. A wooden chopping bowl or food chopper will do equally well. Add brown sugar, juice and spices and mix well. Put to one side. Beat together butter, sugar and egg. Sift flour, baking powder and salt together and add gradually to creamed mixture. Beat well after each addition. This should make a stiff, smooth dough. Divide dough in half, and roll each half thin on floured board. Cut in 3-inch rounds. Measure out 1 teaspoon or more of filling and place in center of each round. Place another round on top of this and seal edges by pressing together with tines of fork or pinching with fingers. Prick top with fork. Repeat until material is used up. If dough outlasts filling, substitute leftover jams or fruits. Bake on greased baking sheet at 350° for 15 minutes. Frost with ½ cup confectioner's sugar mixed with 1 tablespoon cream.

GRANDMA'S MOLASSES DROP CAKES

½ cup butter, softened	1 teaspoon baking soda
1 teaspoon salt	1 cup sour milk
1 cup dark brown sugar	1 teaspoon ginger
1 egg, beaten	1 teaspoon cinnamon
1 cup molasses	4½ cups flour

Cream together softened butter, salt and sugar. When measuring sugar, be sure it's packed firmly into cup. Add beaten egg and molasses. Beat well. Stir soda into sour milk and add this to butter mixture, beating thoroughly. Sift ginger, cinnamon and flour together and stir this in, blending and beating well. Drop from cooking spoon onto greased baking pan, being sure to space drops far enough apart so they will not join when cooking. This will make the cookies round. Bake at 375° for 12 minutes. Cool on racks.

AUNT BARBARA'S FRUIT HERMITS

½ cup butter, softened
½ cup dark brown sugar
½ cup white sugar
1 large egg
¼ cup sour milk
1 teaspoon vanilla flavoring
¾ cup raisins
½ cup sliced dates
¼ cup sliced citron

½ cup chopped nuts
1½ cups flour
¼ teaspoon salt
1 teaspoon baking powder
½ teaspoon baking soda
1 teaspoon cinnamon
¼ teaspoon nutmeg
⅛ teaspoon allspice
⅛ teaspoon cloves

Put softened butter into large mixing bowl. Add sugars and cream well. Add egg, sour milk and vanilla, and beat thoroughly. Then add raisins, dates, citron and nuts. Sift dry ingredients together and stir into first mixture, blending well. Drop by teaspoon onto greased baking pan. Flatten each ball by pressing down with wet knife or spatula. Bake at 375° for 12 minutes. Cool on wire racks before storing. Makes about 3 dozen.

LEMON HONEY COOKIES

½ cup butter
1 cup sugar
½ teaspoon grated lemon peel
1 teaspoon vanilla flavoring

1 egg, well beaten
2 tablespoons sweet milk
2½ cups flour
2 teaspoons baking powder

Cream together butter, sugar, lemon rind and flavoring. Add egg and milk and beat until fluffy. Sift dry ingredients together and add to first mixture. Put onto lightly floured board and roll thin. Cut into rounds. Place on greased baking pan and bake at 375° for 12 minutes. Put 2 cookies together with:

LEMON FILLING

1 tablespoon cornstarch
¼ cup cold water
1 cup sugar

1 tablespoon lemon juice
2 tablespoons butter
1 egg, well beaten

Blend cornstarch and water. Cook, stirring constantly, until clear. Then add sugar, lemon juice and butter. Stir until smooth. Cook 3 minutes, then slowly stir in egg. Cook, slowly stirring all the while, 2 minutes, or until well thickened. Chill before spreading between cookies.

MAPLE-BUTTERNUT FROSTING

2½ cups maple sugar
⅛ teaspoon salt
1¼ cups rich milk

¾ cup butternuts, chopped
very fine
½ teaspoon cinnamon

Boil sugar, salt and milk together until a little taken up in a spoon will form a soft ball in a cup of cold water. When this stage is reached, pour at once into a bowl. Beat hard until creamy and of a spreading consistency. By then it will be cooled. Add the chopped nuts, cinnamon and spread on cake layers.

SAND TARTS

⅔ cup shortening
1¼ cups white sugar
2 eggs, beaten
3 cups flour
1 teaspoon salt

2 teaspoons baking powder
1 teaspoon vanilla flavoring
1 teaspoon lemon flavoring
1 egg white, slightly beaten
¼ cup white sugar

1½ teaspoons cinnamon

Cream together shortening, sugar and eggs. Sift together flour, salt and baking powder. Add these to first mixture and blend thoroughly. Add flavorings and mix to a smooth dough. Roll out thin on a lightly floured board, cutting into squares, rounds, or diamonds with cookie cutters.

Next brush tops of cookies with egg white, sprinkle on sugar and dust with cinnamon. Bake at 325° for 12 to 15 minutes.

Chapter 28

Game

ROAST SADDLE OF VENISON

4-pound saddle of venison	sprig of thyme
2 ounces butter	2 bay leaves
2 small stalks celery	3 cloves
1 large onion	1 teaspoon peppercorns
1 carrot	1 cup rich beef stock

salt and pepper

Rub well-cleaned saddle of deer meat with butter and sprinkle
it with salt and pepper. Place celery, onion, carrot, thyme, bay

leaves, cloves and peppercorns around venison in roasting pan. Roast in a moderately hot oven (325°) for 1½ hours. Baste often with own liquor or gravy. When done lift from pan and place on rack. Using drippings, add stock and reduce it a third, adding a speck of salt and pepper. Keep saddle hot meanwhile, and when ready to serve pour gravy over venison. Serve with wild beach plum jelly.

VENISON STEW

1½ pounds venison	cider vinegar
4 onions, sliced	4 carrots, diced
6 bay leaves	5 stalks celery
salt and pepper	

The deer meat must be marinated to fashion a good stew. To do this, place meat in earthen jar together with onions and bay leaves. Cover with cider vinegar and put jar in cool place for 2 days. Then wash meat in cold water and put it in kettle with boiling water to cover. Stew slowly until meat is tender. Remove from water and bone it. Cook carrots and celery in broth until tender. Cut meat into pieces the size of medium-sized potatoes and add to vegetable and broth mixture. Thicken broth, and flavor with salt and pepper to taste.

BAKED PARTRIDGE

2 dressed partridges	1½ teaspoons salt
¼ cup melted fat	1 teaspoon black pepper
¼ cup crushed juniper berries	¾ cup beef stock

After the hunter brings the birds in, let them age three or four days before using. Then dress them out, singe them well, and wash in cold water. Mix fat and berries and rub birds inside and out with mixture, being sure to cover all parts and leaving a goodly quantity on flesh. Sprinkle with salt and pepper and put into greased baking dish. Roast at 425° until partridges are well browned. Then pour over them ½ cup beef stock, cover dish and reduce heat to 350°. Cook for another hour, using up balance of stock if needed.

In our family partridge was considered the king of game for eating purposes. Grandma said a drumstick from a well-fed hen or cock partridge had more flavor than she had ever found in any other meat. The birds eat berries, nuts and young shoots in the forest and their flesh has a gamy taste that is utterly devastating.

ROAST WILD DUCK

2 wild ducks, singed and washed	2 stalks celery, diced
salt and pepper	2 oranges, seeded and cut up,
2 large apples, cored and	but not peeled
quartered, but not peeled	½ cup melted butter

If the hunter has dressed the ducks well, the cook needs only to wash the birds in cold water and singe them carefully. With old cloth or tea towel wipe ducks inside and out and sprinkle with salt and pepper. Mix apples, celery and oranges together, and into each cavity put half of mixture. Rub birds all over thoroughly with melted butter. Place ducks in open roasting pan and bake in very hot oven (450°) for 20 minutes. Baste frequently with melted butter. Reduce heat to 350° and roast for another hour. This time cover dish. If you prefer duck rare, cut down on the time at the end, testing until it suits you.

WILD GAME SAUCE

3 tablespoons chopped onion
2 tablespoons chopped celery
2 tablespoons chopped parsley
4 tablespoons pan drippings
2 tablespoons flour

¼ teaspoon poultry seasoning
¼ teaspoon black pepper
  salt to taste
½ cup wild beach plum jelly
1 tablespoon lemon juice

1½ cups juices from baking pan

Brown onion, celery, and parsley in pan drippings, using heavy skillet. Blend in flour and stir until browned. Add seasonings, jelly, lemon juice and juices from pan. Often there will not be enough pan drippings to supply 4 tablespoons used above and still have enough for 1½ cups more. In such a situation make up difference with rich meat stock. The pan drippings will give a more piquant taste than beef stock, so utilize all there is.

Blend all ingredients together smoothly, and simmer for a few minutes. Sauce for wild game should not be thick like gravy. This one is excellent for partridge, wild duck, roast venison or pheasant.

RABBIT POT PIE

1 rabbit, cleaned and cut in
  pieces
1 teaspoon salt
1 large celery stalk
1 large onion
2 peppercorns
1 bay leaf
1 sprig parsley
  boiling water

1½ cups small white onions
8 carrots, diced
2 cups green peas
1 cup diced white potatoes
2 tablespoons flour
½ cup milk
1 tablespoon butter
1 unbaked pastry top (see
  page 165)

salt and pepper

Wash rabbit pieces, place them in kettle with salt, celery, large onion, peppercorns, bay leaf and parsley. Cover with boiling water, put lid on dish and simmer gently until rabbit meat is tender. Drain and strain liquor, saving clear liquid. Remove meat from the bones and lay by. Before cooking rabbit or afterwards, as the case may be, cook items in right-hand column in this fashion:

Boil white onions, carrots, peas and potatoes until done. Mix together lightly. Thicken rabbit liquor with flour that has been blended with cold water. Add milk and pour all over rabbit meat and vegetables in baking dish. Dot with butter, and season until agreeable to individual taste. Place unbaked pastry over top of pie, being sure to gash it in center so steam may escape. Bake at 425° until crust is brown and entire pie is hot through and through.

Chapter 29

Beverages

MULLED CIDER

1 quart sweet cider	3 whole allspice
5 whole cloves	1 piece stick cinnamon

Mix ingredients together and heat thoroughly over medium fire for 15 minutes. Strain and serve hot. A cinnamon stick as a stirring spoon in the mug is better than a silver spoon.

HUCKLEBERRY FROTH

1 cup huckleberry juice
1½ cups juice from canned
   peaches or pears

juice of 2 lemons
1 cup water
   sugar to taste

Mix ingredients together. Chill thoroughly. Just before serving shake until very frothy.

RASPBERRY SHRUB

4 quarts raspberries
1½ pints cider vinegar

16 cups sugar, to taste best,
   more if desired

Pick over berries carefully, pour vinegar over them and let stand 3 days. Strain through flannel bag, squeezing cloth a little, but not enough to let any pulp through. Add 2 cups sugar to each pint of juice; boil quickly in enamel saucepan for 15 minutes. Bottle, cork tightly and keep in cool place. Use 2 tablespoons of shrub per glass of ice water when serving.

MULLED GRAPE JUICE

2 cups grape juice
1 cup water
1 cup sugar

1 stick cinnamon
6 cloves
   juice of 1 lemon

Mix grape juice, water and sugar in saucepan. Tie spices in a little cloth bag and drop into liquid. Bring all to a boil. Stir and allow to stand over *low* heat for 10 minutes. Take out spice bag and add lemon juice. Again bring just to a boil. Serve very hot from an earthenware teapot.

EGG NOG

1 egg yolk	1 cup rich milk
2 tablespoons sugar	1 egg white
1½ teaspoons flavoring	sprinkling of nutmeg

This is for an individual egg nog drink, and can be whipped up quickly. The flavoring may be vanilla, strawberry juice, chocolate, coffee or orange flavoring.

Beat egg yolk until light and add sugar. Beat thoroughly. Add desired flavoring and beat in milk. Beat egg white stiff and fold it in. Pour into tall glass and dust top with grated nutmeg. Serve cold.

Chapter 30

Odds and Ends

AUNT ANNIE'S CHILI SAUCE

18 ripe tomatoes, peeled and
   cut up
2 green peppers, seeded and
   cut up
6 onions, peeled and cut up
1 cup sugar

2½ cups vinegar
2 teaspoons salt
1 teaspoon cinnamon
1 teaspoon allspice
1 teaspoon nutmeg
½ teaspoon ground cloves

Cook tomatoes, peppers and onions together until tender. Then add other ingredients and cook for 15 minutes. Pour into sterilized jars and seal.

OLD-FASHIONED MOLASSES TAFFY

1 cup sugar	1 cup water
¾ cup brown sugar	¼ cup butter
2 cups molasses	⅛ teaspoon baking soda
¼ teaspoon salt	

Cook sugars, molasses and water together until brittle over low heat (270°), stirring frequently to prevent burning. Remove from heat, add butter, soda and salt, stirring just enough to mix. Pour into large greased pan and allow to stand until cool enough to handle. Butter fingers and pull until firm and light yellow. Two can do this better than one. Stretch into a rope, twist and cut into 1-inch lengths. Makes about 50 pieces.

WILD BLACK RASPBERRY JELLY

No detailed list of ingredients is given with this recipe because no one knows how many wild "black caps" will be found when the picking party goes off on the hunt. Anyway, half the fun is in the picking. If there's jelly too, it is like an extra bonus.

Wash and hull as many berries as are brought home and cover with just enough cold water to show through top layer of fruit. Then boil rapidly for 10 minutes. Mash berries and allow juice to *drip* through a clean piece of muslin or a jelly bag. Do not squeeze. Measure resulting juice and allow ¾ cup sugar for each cup of juice. Put liquid in kettle and boil for 4 minutes. Then stir in sugar. Boil syrup until it jells. Grandma tested hers by dropping some syrup from long edge of a cold silver spoon into a saucer. When 2 drops "sheet" off at the same time, it is done. Pour into sterilized jelly glasses, seal with hot paraffin, cover with lids and store in a cool, dark place.

Black raspberry jam can be made from pulp left from jelly

making. Measure pulp, use ¾ cup sugar to each cup of pulp, and mix together. Cook for 20 minutes, stirring constantly. Then seal at once in sterilized containers.

Wild Beach Plum Jelly is made the same way wild raspberry jelly is made except that 1 cup of sugar is needed for each cup of juice.

GREEN TOMATO PRESERVES

4 pounds green tomatoes	1 teaspoon salt
5 lemons	4 cups sugar
1 stick cinnamon	

Wash and stem green tomatoes and remove any blemishes in skin. Peel lemons and cut peel into thin slices. Cover lemon strips with water and cook 5 minutes. Drain and discard liquid. Cut up lemon pulp and remove seeds. Slice green tomatoes very thin. Then combine peel, pulp and tomatoes. Add salt, sugar and cinnamon. Boil rapidly, stirring to prevent scorching, until mixture is thick and tomatoes appear clear. This takes about 20 minutes. Pour into hot, sterilized jars.

SWEET SPICED SECKEL PEARS

8 pounds of Seckel pears	2 cups liquid from pears
water to cover	2 sticks cinnamon
8¼ cups sugar	1 tablespoon whole cloves
2 cups cider vinegar	1 small piece ginger root
2 blades of mace	

Wash pears, remove blossom ends, but do *not* remove stems and do not peel. Use enough water to cover fruit and bring to a boil. Cook for 5 minutes and drain, reserving liquid. In large kettle place sugar, vinegar, 2 cups liquid from cooking pears, and spices. Cook for 5 minutes and then add pears. Cook very slowly until tender. They should become almost transparent. Pack while hot in hot, sterilized jars. Cover with hot syrup and seal at once.

Crab apples and peaches may be prepared in the same way.

Index